D1463620

"To be intentional about creating a ___ of hope is a powerful driver of performance and results…This is much more than a feel-good book about hope. It's a 'how-to' book about putting hope to work in our businesses and in our lives."

—JOE CALLOWAY, author, *Be the Best at What Matters Most*

"Libby Gill has done it again, though we should hardly be surprised. She's an amazing mentor and teacher, as well as a practitioner! In this book, she shows us why the concept of hope is significantly different from what most think it is, and how we can utilize it correctly, strategically, and methodically in order to become the best leader we can be and add exceptional value to the lives of everyone we touch!"

—BOB BURG, co-author of *The Go-Giver*
and *The Go-Giver Influencer*

"In *The Hope-Driven Leader*, Libby Gill expertly guides readers through actionable steps and exercises to bring hope into their lives and the lives of others. Whether you are a business leader, a community leader, or simply want to foster hope within your own family, *The Hope-Driven Leader* is a must-read."

—LOUIS EFRON, *Forbes* and *HuffPost* contributor
and author of *Purpose Meets Execution* and
How to Find a Job, Career and Life You Love

"Every tribe deserves a leader who inspires its members with hope. At the WD-40 Company, our main purpose is to create positive, lasting memories even as we build a better future. In her new book, Libby Gill gives practical advice on how to advance your organization using hope as an essential tool in your kit. When you begin with hope—for your customers and tribe members alike—your future becomes expansive with new perspectives and fresh possibilities."

—GARRY RIDGE, CEO, WD-40 Company, author,
*Helping People Win at Work: A Business Philosophy Called
"Don't Mark My Paper, Help Me Get an A"* with Ken Blanchard

"Having HOPE is something we all struggle with at some point in our lives. It's comforting to know that others have fought this same battle and have come out the other side, happier, healthier and yes, more hopeful. This is a book for anyone who dreams big, cares for others as well as themselves and who fearlessly tackles each day as it comes."

—TRACEY NOONAN, CEO & Co-Founder
of Wicked Good Cupcakes, Inc.

"Libby Gill's *The Hope-Driven Leader* is inspiring but also practical. She sparks the reader to find hope, but the book goes beyond just inspiring and shows leaders how to take real action. Using hope to shift mindsets and drive a more productive workplace is a refreshing perspective that many leaders could benefit from reading."

—MARNIE BLACK, Executive Vice President,
Public Relations, AMC & SundanceTV

"Libby Gill's theory of hope is the imagined "yellow brick road" to a personally and professionally fulfilled life…and the guidance to find your path…even if you aren't Dorothy!"

—SUSAN Q. GALLIN, Broadway Producer of hit plays
including Pulitzer Prize-winning *Angels in America*,
Who's Afraid of Virginia Woolf, and *The Heidi Chronicles*

"Hope. That ethereal and ever-elusive component we seek. Libby Gill's *The Hope-Driven Leader* guides the reader through the maze and to that place where hope dwells. The Hope-Driven Leader is a guide for all leaders, may they lead at work, at home, or at heart."

—CATHERINE CARR, Humanitarian, Doctors Without Borders

"The leader that inspires hope in others holds the keys to creating sustainable excellence in today's rapidly and dramatically changing world. In *The Hope-Driven Leader*, Libby Gill shows step by step how to harness the power of positivity at work. Don't miss this opportunity to get the jump on the competition."

—DR. JEFF SPENCER, Former Olympic Cyclist and
Creator of the Goal Achievement Roadmap

THE
HOPE-DRIVEN
LEADER

Harness the Power of
Positivity at Work

LIBBY GILL

DIVERSION
BOOKS

Diversion Books
A Division of Diversion Publishing Corp.
443 Park Avenue South, Suite 1008
New York, New York 10016
www.DiversionBooks.com

Copyright © 2018 by Libby Gill
All rights reserved, including the right to reproduce this book or portions
thereof in any form whatsoever.

For more information, email info@diversionbooks.com

First Diversion Books edition April 2018.
Paperback ISBN: 978-1-63576-375-1
eBook ISBN: 978-1-63576-374-4

LSIDB/1802

CONTENTS

CHAPTER 1

HARNESSING HOPE

Jet Fuel for the Journey of Work and Life

"He who has health has hope.
And he who has hope has everything."
—*Arabic Proverb*

I got my first big career break when I was hired by a television production and distribution company founded by the legendary TV producer Norman Lear, creator of such hits as *All in the Family*. Prior to that, I had knocked around Hollywood for almost a decade, working as a studio temp or production assistant or, one too-hot summer, as a tap dancing bear at a local amusement park. I was beyond thrilled when I landed a job at Lear's Embassy Communications, a job that included a parking space and healthcare benefits. I had finally arrived.

But the dawn of the morning I was scheduled to start as executive assistant to the VP of public relations and promotion, I got a call from my father in Florida that threw off not only my start date, but also my way of looking at the world. My dad had left a message on my answering machine (remember those?) the night before that was so garbled I couldn't tell what he was saying. It was late when I got the message so I decided I would call him in the morning. He called a second time around 5 am to tell me that my stepmother Fran, with whom I'd spent a big portion of my life, had committed suicide.

There was nothing I could do but call the office and tell my new boss that I'd have to start a week later. I didn't tell him the reason. I didn't tell anyone. I just went home to Florida and helped my dad plan a funeral and clean out Fran's closets. When I got back to work the next week, something had changed. The new job and the new boss were exactly as expected, but something felt terribly wrong. *Me.*

I'd come back from Florida—where I'd had a less-than-happy childhood punctuated by a revolving door of stepsiblings, multiple household relocations, and six high schools over the course of six years—feeling lost and broken. I'd suffered the same tragedies as lots of people (okay—maybe more than some), but still I couldn't seem to find my equilibrium. So I did the only thing I knew how to do—*work.*

It was as if Fran's suicide had woken me to the fact that time was precious and I didn't want to waste it on bad decisions, unsatisfying relationships, or work that didn't fulfill me. But I felt so powerless in my little job and my little apartment; I had no idea what or how to change. One particularly lonely night several months after Fran had died, my roommate was away for the weekend and I wandered into the kitchen to look for something that would either numb or comfort me. Neither of us took drugs, so that was out. There wasn't any chocolate in the house, so that wasn't an option. But I found a big bottle of brandy from some long-ago recipe and decided that would have to do the trick.

I downed a glass, then another, then the thought struck me that I had never tried on Fran's mink coat, my sole inheritance, which my father had insisted I take home with me after her funeral. I opened my closet, unzipped the garment bag, and put on the coat. To my great surprise, the weight of that fur, or maybe the weight of my own pain, brought me to my knees. I stumbled, then crawled into the hallway of my apartment, still wrapped in the mink, the bottle of brandy in my hand. I stayed there crying my eyes out for what might have been the entire weekend, grateful that the couple downstairs were deaf and couldn't hear my sobs.

As I lay on the floor, a thought suddenly popped into my head. I had absolutely no idea what the strange phrase meant at the time, but it stuck with me like a mantra for years. *Hope and tools.* About the time I started my own business as an executive coach and leadership consultant, I found myself expanding on that mantra, particularly the hope piece as the one quality no one could afford to be without. The jet fuel for the journey of work and life.

Although I had never intended to pursue public relations as a career, I dug into my new role with a zeal that belied my natural introversion. I worked crazy hours, often dealing with crazy people. But I enjoyed the challenge of learning the entertainment business and assisting my boss in securing press coverage for our executives, stars, and TV series. When one of the staff publicists (oddly enough, also named Libby) decided to leave to start her own firm, I surprised myself by marching into my boss's office and asking for her job.

My boss told me that he planned to interview several candidates, but would be happy to include me in the mix. However, he warned me sternly, if he promoted me to publicist and it didn't work out, my old job would be filled and I'd have to leave the company. "Not a problem," I told him with more confidence than I felt.

I got the job, my first promotion in less than a year. After that, the friendly mid-size company I thought I had joined was bought by Columbia Pictures, then Coca-Cola, and eventually became part of Sony Pictures Entertainment. With each reorganization, I raised my hand and asked for more. Volunteer and figure it out later became my modus operandi.

In just five years, I moved up the corporate food chain from assistant to publicist to manager to director. Just a year later, I took over my old boss's role, albeit on a larger scale, as vice president of publicity, advertising, and promotion for Sony's Worldwide Television Group. Despite my doubts and insecurities about my value (and they were considerable), I felt, I knew—deep inside—that I had the power to improve my life.

It was years before I understood the real significance of *hope*. And that the mysterious mantra—*hope and tools*—that had popped into my head that particularly lonely night would be instrumental in helping propel me, and eventually the people I helped, past the inevitable obstacles we faced on our way to a better future.

WHAT IS HOPE THEORY?

We've all heard the saying "hope is not a strategy." Yet, having motivated and managed people for nearly thirty years, I've observed again and again how ineffective it is to provide people with strategies or resources when they're feeling hopeless. It's like giving a worker a power tool with no electricity. Utterly useless. Instead, by instilling an individual or an organization with a sense of hopefulness, we can guide them to connect the beliefs to the behaviors that will ultimately help them realize their vision.

That's what this book is about: belief driving behavior based on the science of *hope theory*, which stems from a body of research from the medical and positive psychology communities that tells us that *hope*—unlike its emotional cousins *happiness* and *optimism*—is specific, situational, and future focused. Before we go any further, let's take a look at the science of hope theory and what it means to you.

The word *hope* is derived from the Old English word *hopian*, which literally means to "leap forward with expectation." Hope plays such a pivotal part in our lives that scientists have endeavored to define its role and determine how it affects our daily existence. The concept was pioneered by the late Dr. C.R. Snyder, a professor of psychology and, from 1974 to 2001, director of the graduate training program in clinical psychology at the University of Kansas at Lawrence. Encouraged by the noted psychiatrist Dr. Karl Menninger, who once spoke about hope at a conference of the American Psychiatric Association (only to have his concepts derided by his colleagues), Dr. Snyder became intrigued with the significance of hope and its role in helping us reach our goals.[1]

WILLPOWER AND WAYPOWER

Snyder defined *hope* as based on both "willpower" and "waypower," where one is able not only to create the pathways to realizing a vision, but also to sustain the mental energy and perseverance to travel those pathways effectively. He likened this process to the saying "where's a will, there's a way," citing both elements as critical to success. Today, with the world and workplace focused on ideas and innovation rather than merely output, the most successful people are often the most hopeful. One of the primary reasons is because they see *multiple* pathways, rather than *the* way, to arrive at a successful outcome.

Dr. Snyder's research demonstrates that people with a high level of hope (not to be confused with optimism, which is a generalized outlook on life independent of one's actions and circumstances), are more likely than non-hopeful people to:

- Set a great number of goals
- Have goals that may be more difficult to attain

---

1   C.R. Snyder, *The Psychology of Hope: You Can Get Here from There* (New York: The Free Press, 1994).

- Be more successful at reaching their goals
- Have less distress and greater happiness than low-hope people

BELIEF AND EXPECTATION

Adding to the pioneering work of Dr. Snyder is Harvard-trained oncologist Dr. Jerome Groopman, one of the world's leading researchers on cancer and AIDS. Author of *How Doctors Think* and *The Anatomy of Hope*, Dr. Groopman believes that hope consists of two key components: belief and expectation. More specifically, belief that change is possible and the expectation that the actions of an individual can result in a better future.

As a clinician, Dr. Groopman learned that when he gave cancer patients too much information regarding their prognosis, he often robbed them of hopefulness, which he and many other scientists believe is instrumental in the healing process. On the other hand, when he gave them too limited information, he ran the risk of creating the false impression that they had little about which to be concerned. It was the challenge of finding that delicate balance between *true hope* and *false hope* that propelled Dr. Groopman to advance the research in the field of hope theory. What Groopman's research makes clear is that, unlike wishfulness or positive thinking (without action), hope can have a physiological impact on the brain, releasing powerful chemicals like enkephalins and endorphins that help us endure pain and boost our immune system.[2]

---

2 Jerome Groopman, *The Anatomy of Hope: How People Prevail in the Face of Illness* (New York: Random House, 2004).

HOW BELIEF DRIVES BEHAVIOR

Although Snyder and Groopman approached hope theory from different perspectives—medicine and psychology—it is clear that both saw it as a combination of feelings and actions. Or, as I see it, it is the interconnection between beliefs and behaviors. If you believe that change is possible and that your actions will have a positive influence on outcomes, you're less likely to defend the status quo and more likely to take positive risks, inspiring others with your behavior. Conversely, if you believe the opposite is true, that change is impossible and it makes absolutely no difference what actions you take, you're apt to stay stuck in mediocrity. Or, as Henry Ford famously put it, "Whether you think you can or think you can't, you're right."

So why are some people and companies eternally energized with a sense of hopefulness, while others are perpetually stuck in the hope-starved doldrums? How do some leaders manage to inspire an anything-is-possible confidence in their teams, while others struggle to keep employees even marginally engaged? How do some people stay so connected to their vision that even serious setbacks like illness, loss of a loved one, or a job layoff don't deter them?

ARE YOU SETTLING FOR SECOND BEST?

As I found my path in the professional world, I was proud that I had discovered an area in which I could excel, yet some nagging voice in the back of my head continued to remind me that PR wasn't what I really wanted to do. I wanted to work as a writer or in a creative role in film or television. Yet, I cancelled interviews and shied away from connections that could have furthered that goal, convincing myself that no one would ever hire me for my skills or talent. Instead, I settled for second best. Not that public relations was a bad career choice. It allowed me to buy a house, care for my family, and come in contact with some truly brilliant people. But if I asked myself (which I rarely did) what I wanted to do with my life, a career in PR wasn't even on the list. I had let fear become my guide.

It took me until my mid-forties to figure out who I was and what I wanted in my personal and professional life. Having survived a tumultuous childhood and a rocky young adulthood, I'd come out the other side and had the battle scars to prove it. Eventually, the old me just didn't fit anymore. In just one year, I left my corporate job, started my own business, published my first book, got divorced, lost thirty pounds, and started over. It wasn't an easy year, and I don't wish that on you. Rather, my goal with this book is to offer you a roadmap in how hope can fuel the positive beliefs and drive the meaningful behaviors that get you where you want to go.

We often hear the term "settling" regarding romantic relationships. Did you *settle* for your significant other because you didn't want to be alone? Did you *settle* because it was simply too frightening to go out and find someone new? Or did you *settle* because not doing so would mean that you'd have to look at yourself under the microscope and see what you needed to fix about you?

Settling can happen in any part of your life: work, family, health, finances. Not that you can control every event. Bad things really do happen to good people. But if you know there's more you can do, have, or become and you don't strive for it, then perhaps, you deserve what you get. Harsh, I know, but that's the reality. Ask yourself if you have ever experienced any of these signals that you're settling.

SEVEN SIGNALS THAT YOU'RE SETTLING

1. You have a dream or goal stuck way in the back of your head, but you never seem to take any action toward it. Maybe it's changing careers, starting a business, having a child, or running a marathon. It's like an earworm, also known as *stuck song syndrome* or *musical imagery repetition* (and, no, I didn't make up those terms), that catchy melody or unforgettable lyric that you can't get out of your mind long after the music stops playing. You try to ignore it, but it's always in the background, drumming that beat in your head and heart.

2. You're living the *someday syndrome*, keeping your goal in the later-on-in-life category. Guess what? You don't know how long you have on this earth. Do you really want to wait around to see if you manage to squeeze in something you know in your heart of hearts is truly meaningful to you?

3. You've let the green-eyed monster of envy and jealousy take up permanent residence in your gut. When you see other people succeeding, you find some way to attribute it to their education,

money, nepotism, or just dumb luck. You tell yourself that they have all the advantages that you don't. Even if some or all of those beliefs are true, so what? By convincing yourself that if only you had all the great stuff those successful people do, you'd be successful, too, you're letting yourself off the hook from facing the reality of your situation—whatever it is—and doing the work that will get you where you want to be.

4. You've got a *shrink-to-fit personality.* You may have big dreams, but you tell yourself they're just not realistic. Instead, it's okay to keep plugging away at this safe, boring, little job. Or to stick with playing small rather than risk ruffling anyone else's feathers—or worse, risk failing at something. You're like those amusement park Whack-a-Moles: if you just stay safely underground, no one can ever smack you back down.

5. You're a *substitution junkie.* Rather than get your high by fulfilling your dreams, you become obsessed with food, alcohol, television, news, social media, or other diversions. Don't get me wrong. I'm a food and wine person of the first order, but I don't kid myself that earthly pleasures (including TV and movies, two more of my favs) are any kind of substitute for purposeful work or meaningful relationships.

6. You're a perpetual blamer of others. If you can't have what you really want, it's somebody else's fault. It's your boss holding you back. Or the government, the job market, your childhood or

spouse. You can find a million excuses outside yourself for not getting what you want, but you know that the only one to blame is you.

7. You're *hope starved*. Rather than feeding on positive ideas and inspiring people, you let the negatives of the world—and there are plenty of them—become your constant diet. You tell yourself that you don't have what it takes, you don't know how to get ahead, you don't have the right skills or certifications, you're too old, too young, too dumb, too smart, or too whatever. The truth is you've let your positive vision of the future get buried under other people's negative rubble. It's time to start digging out.

Awareness that you're settling for less than you deserve could be the kick in the rear end you need to start focusing on what you really want. And even if you don't particularly feel like you're settling, let's see how the practice of mentally connecting our present to our future can help us realize our vision.

DON'T STOP THINKING ABOUT TOMORROW

We hear a lot about living in the moment. And while single-minded focus on the present is a great tool for productivity as well as relaxation, it's critical that we also live in the future. In his book *Personal Intelligence: The Power of Personality and How It Shapes Our Lives,* renowned psychologist John D. Mayer, one of the originators of the concept of emotional intelligence, theorizes that the more vividly we can imagine our future selves, the more similar we become to the self we imagine.[3]

In studying the differences between people who focus more on the present and those who focus on the future, former Stanford psychologists Philip G. Zimbardo and John N. Boyd discovered that present-focused people tended to experience more spontaneity and freedom but were also more prone to high-risk behaviors like substance abuse than their future-focused counterparts. By contrast, people who are more mindful of the future, particularly when that future is realistic and attainable, tend to take greater stewardship over their present lives so they can reach the future they've imagined.

How closely we are able to align our present selves with our future selves can be a major indicator of the degree of success we experience. In another Stanford experiment, Hal Ersner-Hershfield devised a simple method of measuring this alignment. He gave study participants a diagram with seven pairs of circles marked "Present Self" and "Future Self." The first two circles did not overlap, indicating that there was little or no connection between those two selves, while subsequent pairs overlapped more and more. The final pair of circles overlapped significantly, showing a close connection between selves. The participants were asked to identify which set of circles most closely resembled how

---

3 John D. Mayer, *Personal Intelligence: The Power of Personality and How It Shapes Our Lives* (New York: Scientific American/Farrar, Straus and Giroux, 2014).

they saw themselves in terms of who they were now and who they realistically hoped to become. Not surprisingly, the people who felt most aligned with their future selves tended to make better long-term decisions, whether related to amassing wealth or taking care of their health. Hope, with its emphasis on belief driving behavior, is the critical component that links present to future. As you read through this book, think about the beliefs and behaviors that will help you close the gap between who you are today and who you want to be tomorrow.[4]

HOPEFUL HABITS

At the end of every chapter of *The Hope-Driven Leader*, you'll find a section called *Hopeful Habits* that includes a top-line summary of the key takeaway from the chapter, and a positive concept summed up as a *Hopeful Belief* for you to ponder, accept or adapt (or reject) as you see fit. Following that, you'll see an accompanying *Hopeful Behavior* that will translate that idea into action. While it's great to understand these concepts intellectually, it's only by seeing what works for you, and then making those behaviors habitual, that you will begin to experience exponential growth and change. Good luck on your road to hopeful discovery.

KEY TAKEAWAY #1

4 John D. Mayer, "How to Plan for Your Future Self," *Scientific American*, March 1, 2014, https://www.scientificamerican.com/article/how-to-plan-for-your-future-self/.

Hope is the jet fuel for the journey of work and life. While we've been taught to believe that "hope is not a strategy," hope must be present *before* the application of strategies and resources for us to make full use of the tools that lead to positive change.

HOPEFUL BELIEF #1

Now that we've seen how critical (and scientifically valid) it is to link your current life with your future goals, let's begin to visualize that future self. We can start by putting a twist on the question we've all been asked as kids. Instead of "*What* do you want to be when you grow up?" ask yourself, "*Who* do you want to be when you grow up?"

What positive personality traits do you currently see in yourself that you'd like to develop over time? These might include being adventurous, intellectually curious, health minded, and/or financially savvy. Now, ask yourself the opposite. What less appealing traits would you like to minimize over time? These could include overspending, bad nutrition or exercise habits, and/or reluctance to go after the promotion or job you want. In other words, begin to imagine the next iteration of you. Be aware of the gap and what you need to do to close it.

HOPEFUL BEHAVIOR #1

Pick one positive trait that you currently see as part of your personality. Now, add an action that would amplify the positive trait. For example, if you said you wanted to develop your intellectual curiosity, you might consider taking a class, attending a seminar, or listening to an audio series that would expand your skills or knowledge.

Next, pick the negative trait you wish to minimize over time. If you determined that your finance savvy is not up to par, pick an action that would begin to build that muscle. Perhaps you'll decide to meet with an investment advisor, overhaul your college or retirement plans, or take a seminar in financial planning. By consciously focusing on your beliefs, both positive and negative, you can begin to identify behaviors to expand and develop your best future self.

In chapter two, we'll take a look at the history of hope to see how the concept has developed in literature and theology over time.

CHAPTER 2

WHAT'S HOPE GOT TO DO WITH IT?

The Science and Significance of Hope Theory

"Hope is the dream of a waking man."
—*Aristotle*

You probably know the story of the first man and woman from the Bible's Book of Genesis, Adam and Eve. But you may not be as familiar with the Greek myth about the first woman: Pandora.

In *Works and Days,* written by eighth century BC Greek poet Hesiod, he talks about the Golden Age when men were immortal and dwelled on Olympus, which ended when Prometheus stole fire and brought it down to Earth. Zeus, the supreme god of the Olympians, was so angry he had Hephaistos, the Greek god of smiths and craftsmen, fashion a beautiful and cunning woman out of clay, and sent her to Earth to become the bride of Prometheus's foolish younger brother, Epimetheus.

Prometheus, fearing retribution from Zeus for his theft of fire, warned his brother not to accept anything from Zeus. However, Epimetheus ignored him and took Pandora as his bride, along with Zeus's wedding gift of a storage jar (later described as a box). Unable to resist her curiosity, Pandora promptly opened the jar, unleashing all manner of evil spirits to plague mankind forever. Seeing what she'd done, Pandora swiftly slammed the lid of the jar shut, but it was too late. To make matters worse, she trapped only one remaining spirit inside the jar: *hope*.

There's some surprisingly lively debate among classics scholars and historians about whether hope was sealed inside the jar to ensure man's suffering or to mitigate it. As a hopeful, half-full kind of person, I prefer to think that rather than withholding hope, the gods offered it as an antidote for our worldly ills.

In this chapter, we'll look at the science and history of hope theory to shed some light on its origins, as well as its applications to your life.

WHAT IS HOPE?

Though their definitions may differ, the idea of hope has resonated with writers, poets, philosophers, and theologians for centuries. In some religions, hope is considered a necessary ingredient for an individual or group to reach heaven. In others, hope is the spiritual byproduct, a gift given to those who live lives of piety.

In the Christian religion, the three "theological virtues"—hope, faith, and charity—are cited as the traits needed to live a good and moral life. Unlike the cardinal or moral virtues (prudence, justice, fortitude, and temperance), which may be practiced by anyone, the theological virtues are thought to be God-given. Hope is cited more than one hundred times in the King James Bible, its meaning spanning from trust to deliverance from enemies. Not coincidentally, it is also the basic theme for many of the Negro spirituals passed down among slaves.

In Hindu literature, hope is referred to as "Pradithi" or "Apeksh" and typically refers to desire and expectation. The Hindu book of *Vishnu Smriti*, a holy text of prose and verse told in one hundred chapters, contains a dialogue between the god Vishnu and the goddess Earth, or Prithvi, after Vishnu rescues Earth from the sea. Vishnu Smriti is usually depicted as a man of virtue riding in a chariot toward his desired goal. The chariot is a symbol of hope drawn by the five senses, steering toward bliss and away from greed or anger.

There are also references to hope throughout the realm of secular literature from around the world. One of the most famous, and my favorite, appears in Emily Dickinson's poem "Hope is the thing with feathers (254)." Soaring and magical, her elegant avian metaphor resonates with the uplifting sense of what is possible, but also expresses the tenacity needed to hold tightly to our vision.

Hope is the thing with feathers
That perches in the soul,
And sings the tune without the words,
And never stops at all,

And sweetest in the gale is heard;
And sore must be the storm
That could abash the little bird
That kept so many warm.

I've heard it in the chillest land,
And on the strangest sea;
Yet, never, in extremity,
It asked a crumb of me.[1]

Scores of academics have analyzed this beautiful poem, most concluding that Dickinson's bird is a metaphor for hope that resides perpetually within the soul, riding out challenges, including storms, sea, and chill, asking for nothing in return. It's just one literary reference of hope, along with scores of others from William Shakespeare to Charles Dickens to Cheryl Strayed.

But for every hope-besotted philosopher or writer, there are as many detractors, deriding hopefulness as so much wishful thinking. Like the ever-practical Benjamin Franklin, who wrote in *Poor Richard's Almanac*, "He that lives upon hope will die fasting." Or statesman Francis Bacon, who said, "Hope is a good breakfast, but a bad

---

1   Emily Dickinson, public domain.

supper." Prophetic, perhaps, since Bacon died in disgrace and debt.

Now that we've taken a brief look at hope in religious and literary lore, let's take a look at the science of hope.

HOPE AND POSITIVE PSYCHOLOGY

Stop reading, close your eyes, and imagine your future. What do you see?

That was the question that Dr. Snyder asked in his groundbreaking book *The Psychology of Hope: You Can Get There from Here*. The pioneer of hope theory, Dr. Snyder (now deceased) saw hope as an active state where you determine, through thousands of decisions, how you will get from point A (where you are now) to point B (where you want to go next).[2]

Ironically, it was a poem by Samuel Taylor Coleridge that initially spurred Dr. Snyder's academic study of hope. Coleridge's poem "Work Without Hope" ends with the lines: "Work without Hope draws nectar in a sieve, / And Hope without an object cannot live." The idea, Snyder said, that hope requires an object—or an action—dovetailed with his own thoughts that hope needs to be anchored to a specific goal. Personally, I like Coleridge's comparison of work without hope to nectar in a sieve, something that would give any good manager pause. Maybe Coleridge was onto workplace engagement and productivity way back in the 1800s.

---

2 C.R. Snyder, *The Psychology of Hope: You Can Get There from Here* (New York: The Free Press, 1994).

In *The Psychology of Hope,* Dr. Snyder explains how his hope research began in earnest when he was on sabbatical and went to his university library to check out books on the subject. Discovering that there weren't any, he realized that while philosophers and poets had tackled the subject for centuries, academics and scientists had steered clear, presumably because there was no empirical way to measure it. Undeterred, Dr. Snyder went on to create the Hope Scale to measure low, average, and high levels of hope in thousands of people.

I'll share the Hope Scale with you a little later in the chapter, but first it might be helpful to understand how hope theory defines what hope *is* and what it *isn't.* According to Dr. Snyder, hope consists of three key elements:[3]

- Goals
- Agency
- Pathways

The **goals** Snyder was referring to are not the small or insignificant ones that you can easily achieve without a lot of energy or determination, but rather the significant objects, experiences, or accomplishments that you desire. In other words, a goal is something you want to obtain (like an object) or attain (like an achievement). Typically, the more important a goal is to you, the more mental energy, or willpower, you put into pursuing it. Conversely, if your goal is fuzzy, vague, or simply not that exciting, it's unlikely

---

3 C.R. Snyder et al., "Development and Validation of the State Hope Scale," *Journal of Personality and Social Psychology* 70 (1996): 321–35.

that you will muster up enough energy to stay the course, particularly if you've set a high bar for your goal. (We'll get into vision mapping and goal setting as you create your own roadmap in chapter ten.)

Agency is our ability to take action, to get stuff done. Or as one of my more colorful business acquaintances declares proudly on everything from his company's coffee mugs to t-shirts, "We make sh*t happen." This entrepreneur feels so strongly about getting out of doubt and into action that slightly naughty phrase has become their motto. In the corporate world, we tend to think of those movers and shakers as change agents. Agency, then, is the ability to become masters of our own destiny through the actions we take.

Pathways are the multiple routes to realizing our goals, including planning and prioritizing, working through obstacles, and monitoring our progress. In the Industrial Age, there was often only one way to speed up progress—make the assembly lines go faster. Punitive actions like docking pay and cancelling breaks were often used as employee motivators. But now that we live in the Information Age, or more aptly, the Imagination Age, there are frequently multiple pathways to achieving success. When individuals can strategize numerous routes to their end goal, they are far more likely to persist even when faced with challenges and setbacks.

What hope *isn't* is optimism, wishful thinking, the law of attraction, or happiness. Let's look at optimism first. Optimism is the assumption of a positive outcome—not in itself a bad thing—absent the actions that will create that outcome. Hope, on the other hand, is the assumption of a positive outcome *coupled* with the situation-specific actions and behaviors that will get you to that outcome. Apparently, there is no global shortage of optimism—according to a 2008 Gallup World Poll, 89% of those surveyed expect their lives to be as good or better in five years than they are currently.

Wishful thinking, and its popular offshoot the *law of attraction*, is the pleasant indulgence in daydreams like having the ideal job land in your lap, finding the perfect mate, or winning an Academy Award. Nice to fantasize about, but if you're anything like me, you may find it hard to believe that those magical moments have any basis in reality. Swap out those pipe dreams for realistic goals, anticipate the obstacles, take meaningful action, and you've got a far better shot at getting where you want to go.

That brings us to happiness, which has probably been the subject of more study in the past decade than in the past century. Dr. Ed Diener has been dubbed "Dr. Happiness" for his twenty-five-plus years of research in the field of subjective well-being, or the aspect of happiness that can be measured empirically. His characterization of a happy person is one who is generally satisfied with life, is experiencing positive emotions and not experiencing negative emotions. While there's clearly a link between happiness and hope—it's hard to be happy *and* hopeless—hope seems to be more the driving force and happiness the result.[4]

Interestingly, there seems to be a very high correlation between hope and productivity based on research on business outcomes, academic success, and overall well-being. Again, there is powerful evidence that suggests that how

---

4   The Pursuit of Happiness, "Ed Diener," *The Pursuit of Happiness*, accessed July 1, 2017, http://www.pursuit-of-happiness.org/history-of-happiness/ed-diener/.

we think about the future is a strong predictor of how well we'll do in work, school, and life. Dr. Shane Lopez, a student of Dr. C.R. "Rick" Snyder and former professor at the University of Kansas, found that when other conditions were equal, people who scored high on hope had academic scores that were 12% higher than their low-hope counterparts, a 14% increase in business results, and 10% higher happiness scores.[5]

In perhaps the most demonstrable—and dramatic—link of hope to one's vision of the future, Dr. Stephen Stern of the University of Texas in San Antonio studied the relationship between hopelessness and mortality to see if he and his colleagues could predict why some people lived longer than others when health and trauma were not at issue. Dr. Stern's 795 study subjects were elderly Mexican-Americans and European-Americans between the ages of sixty-four and seventy-nine living in San Antonio. When he asked his participants if they were "hopeful about the future," 722, or 91%, of the respondents said "yes," while 73 people, or 9%, answered "no." Not surprisingly, those higher in hope were more likely to exercise and to be more social, while the low-hope participants were more likely to be smokers and to be depressed.

The researchers gave no health or lifestyle advice and had no further contact with the subjects after the initial study, but continued to follow them through their Social Security Numbers and mortality statistics. Astonishingly, just five years later, 29% of the group identified as hope-

---

5 Shane J. Lopez, *Making Hope Happen: Create the Future You Want for Yourself and Others* (New York: Atria Paperback, 2013).

less had died, while only 11% of the hopeful participants had passed away. When all other factors, such as drinking, perceived health, number of illnesses, etc., were statistically controlled, the study showed that those who felt hopeless were twice as likely to die during the follow-up period than those who felt hopeful about the future.[6]

BELIEF AND EXPECTATION

Other than my personal conviction that hope is the driving force of work and life, it was the story of oncologist Dr. Jerome Groopman's clinical discoveries as well as his own struggles with illness that got me hooked on hope. In *The Anatomy of Hope*, Dr. Groopman discusses his shift in thinking about the use of placebos in healthcare, initially considering them a sort of medical sleight of hand but later seeing their potency in contributing to the healing process. The word *placebo* comes from the Latin, meaning "I shall please," and was the term used to describe the work of paid mourners at the Catholic vesper service for the dead, literally pleasing the bereaved with their mournful demonstrations.

Among other research, Groopman describes a study done at Baylor University in Houston regarding placebos and arthroscopic knee surgery. The idea of using placebos became relevant during the 1950s when many clinical trials were done using blind control groups to study the efficacy of a drug or treatment protocol. One of the most common

6   Stephen L. Stern, R. Dhanda, and H.P. Hazuda, "Hopelessness Predicts Mortality in Older Mexican and European Americans," *Psychosomatic Medicine* 63, no. 3 (June 2001): 344–51.

procedures in the country, there are approximately 650,000 knee surgeries per year.

The Baylor study was meant to determine the effects of a placebo surgery versus an actual surgery. In the study, the researchers took a group of potential knee surgery patients and split them into three different subgroups. Two groups got actual surgical treatment—either by *debridement*, where the degenerated cartilage was cut away, or by *lavage*, where the inflamed cells were flushed out with saline. Another group was given a placebo treatment, painstakingly mimicking the actual surgeries, but without any actual surgery taking place. This group went through the same protocol for pre-op as the surgical groups, the same OR treatment with the draping and the medical team calling for instruments, and the same post-op treatment, including an overnight stay in the hospital where they were administered to by the nursing staff who had no idea what group they were in.

What do you suppose was the result?

The two groups that had the surgeries and the group that had the placebo treatment had virtually the same long-term results. This wasn't some kind of woo-woo mysticism or mind-over-matter exercise. On the contrary, what this precisely controlled study showed was that the patients in the placebo group released brain chemicals including endorphins and enkephalins—natural pain suppressants and mood lifters—that allowed them to go through the physical rehab that was necessary to restore the health of their knees.

Dr. Groopman believes that these patients were able to successfully undergo the physical therapy because they had hope—that is, **belief** in a positive result that allowed them to facilitate their own recovery. Additionally, it was the **expectation** that the process itself would be success-ful, as people in white lab coats with hospital badges and authoritative perspectives treated the patients as though they would be cured.

Imagine instead if the placebo study patients had been told, "You're not going to get any real medical treatment, but we'll see how you do in rehab anyway." What do you think might have happened? Odds are they would have shut down because of the pain as well as the lack of belief in the process. But because of their hope—the belief and expectation of a positive outcome—they were able to handle the pain and the rehab.[7]

TRUE HOPE AND FALSE HOPE

Through his years of giving clinical diagnoses and his study of the power of hope, Dr. Groopman concluded that there are actually two types of hope—*true hope* and *false hope*. As a hematologist-oncologist, Groopman shares that in his early career he found himself, intending to be helpful, giving patients so much information about their prognosis that they shut down in fear and overwhelm, unable to muster the hope that could help them in their healing process.

When he saw the results he was getting, Groopman changed his tactic and went to the other end of the spec-trum, withholding data from patients and their families in order not to overload them, only to discover that this gave them a sense of false hope that they would get better even

---

7   Jerome Groopman, *The Anatomy of Hope: How People Prevail in the Face of Illness* (New York: Random House, 2004).

when that outcome was unlikely. What Dr. Groopman eventually found was the sweet spot of *true hope,* where one faces reality dead-on, factors in all the challenges and difficulties, and continues to move forward with the expectation of a positive result.

I see the dynamic of *true hope* versus *false hope* play out among my coaching clients. Recently, a woman I'll call Carol approached me for advice on a business model she had created for promoting alternative healthcare, such as acupuncture, aromatherapy, and so on. Although her practitioners were highly respected in their fields, her business model didn't compensate them—or her—adequately and she had been steadily losing money for seven years.

I recommended that she overhaul her financial model, make some cuts, and start fresh. She insisted it was just a matter of time before she got the bugs out and decided to stick with the business as it was. I heard from her again two years later when she wanted me to help her craft the communications to close down her business. She was a victim of *false hope,* refusing to remove her rose-colored glasses long enough to make the appropriate course corrections. I felt bad for her, but not surprised. Had her beliefs and behaviors been grounded in *true hope,* she would have recognized not only the possibilities but also the pitfalls she was facing and made the changes essential to turning her business around.

MEASURING HOPE

Even if you've never thought of the people who face enormous difficulties in their own lives as having lives rich in hope and happiness, there are many trailblazers that I consider the *heroes of hope*. Take, for example, Helen Keller, who, in 1904, became the first deaf-blind person to earn a college degree. Despite the physical and learning challenges she faced, nearly insurmountable in her time, she graduated from Radcliffe, now part of Harvard, and went on to become a beloved author and activist. Or Stephen Hawking, who was told he had only two years to live because of his ALS disease, yet went on to have a long career as a theoretical physicist, author, and teacher. Or, in what is perhaps one of the most dramatic examples of hope in action I've yet to discover, Dr. Viktor Frankl, a Viennese psychiatrist who survived the notorious Auschwitz and Dachau Nazi death camps to write one of the most instructive and hopeful books of all time, *Man's Search for Meaning*.

If you think those intrepid purveyors of hope are made of hardier stuff than the rest of us, think about the everyday heroes of hope in your life. The people who never seem to run out of time or energy to help other people with advice or connections. Or the people who light up a room with their positive attitudes, no matter what's happening in their own lives. Like my friend mystery writer Shela Dean's eighty-six-year-old aunt Hazel. Despite surviving breast cancer and a stroke, having lost one son to AIDS and the other to suicide, when you ask Hazel how she's doing, you'll get an enthusiastic, "I'm doing great!" This is not another example of rose-colored false hope. Hazel understands life's challenges all too well. But she has big plans like entertaining friends, attending theater and concerts, and traveling abroad. And she's not about to let the hardships and setbacks keep her from living a full life.

As you can see from Hazel's attitude of positivity, some people are capable of persevering when faced with extreme adversity. Others lose heart and back down, even when the circumstances are far less dire. Interestingly, there's actually a numerical scale, Dr. Snyder's *Adult Dispositional Hope Scale,* that gives an indication of just how hopeful you are.[8] Let's take a look.

THE ADULT DISPOSITIONAL HOPE SCALE

The first assessment designed to measure hope, this tool was created by Dr. Rick Snyder and looks at the inherent levels of hope in adults over age 15. The questionnaire consists of twelve questions that consider agency *(I energetically pursue my goals)* and pathways *(I can think of lots of ways out of a jam)*, as well as hope overall.

After you answer the questions, you can score yourself on three separate scales: the agency score, the pathways score, and your overall hope score, which is the sum of the agency and pathways scores. The overall hope score ranges from a minimum of 8 to a maximum of 64, with agency and pathways scores ranging from a minimum of 4 and a maximum of 32. The higher the scores, the higher the level of hope in each of the three areas. Give the Hope Scale a try and see where you fall.

---

8   C.R. Snyder et al., "Development and Validation of the State Hope Scale," Journal of Personality and Social Psychology 70 (1996): 321–35.

Directions

Read each item carefully. Using the scale below, select the number that best describes YOU and write that number down.

1. = Definitely False   5. = Slightly True
2. = Mostly False   6. = Somewhat True
3. = Somewhat False   7. = Mostly True
4. = Slightly False   8. = Definitely True

____ 1. I can think of many ways to get out of a jam.
____ 2. I energetically pursue my goals.
____ 3. I feel tired most of the time.
____ 4. There are lots of ways around any problem.
____ 5. I am easily beat* in an argument.
____ 6. I can think of many ways to get the things in life that are important to me.
____ 7. I worry about my health.
____ 8. Even when others get discouraged, I know I can find a way to solve the problem.
____ 9. My past experiences have prepared me well for my future.
____10. I've been pretty successful in life.
____11. I usually find myself worrying about something.
____12. I meet the goals that I set for myself.

Scoring

- Add up your scores for items 2, 9, 10, and 12. This gives you your agency score, which represents your ability to take action.

- Next, add up scores for items 1, 4, 6, and 8, which make up the pathways subscale. This measures your ability to find multiple means of reaching a desired goal.
- Finally, add your agency and pathways scores together to get your overall hope score.

* I changed Dr. Snyder's word "downed" to "beat" since I discovered that some people have a hard time with Snyder's meaning with that word.[9]

TRY THIS HOME-BASED HOPE TEST

Claremont Graduate University in Claremont, California, was the first educational institution to offer a PhD in positive psychology. Dr. Mihaly Csikszentmihalyi (pronounced CHICK-sent-me-high-ee), creator of flow theory, heads the program, which stresses serious research and development of methods that institutions and organizations can use to enrich people's lives.

To further the field of positive psychology, Dr. Csikszentmihalyi has created research techniques specific to its study. One such technique is the "experience sampling method," which consists of tracking hundreds of subjects over the course of a week. Researchers page or call the subjects at various times to ask how they are feeling at that moment. The responses are then correlated with the subjects' activities, companions, and physical settings.

9 C.R. Snyder et al., "Development and Validation of the State Hope Scale," *Journal of Personality and Social Psychology* 70 (1996): 321–35.

Contrary to people's *beliefs* about what makes them happy, Dr. Csikszentmihalyi says the sampling method shows the *reality* of what they're experiencing and how happy or unhappy it makes them. For example, a grad student who tells herself that she is sick of her studies might realize that it is her vision and passion for her future career that keep her on course. Or a man who tells himself he loves his job may discover it's more limiting than he allows himself to believe.

Why not put this sampling method to the test in an adapted format so you can see what your hope levels are like at different points in your day? Randomly pick three different times of day over the course of a week that will serve as your times to check in on your own emotional experience. Make sure the twenty-one times are varied and reflect different environments and activities in your life. Write those times down in a journal or tablet.

Next, decide on a method of check-in. Try setting the alarm on your cell phone or computer, writing the times in your calendar, or asking someone to call or text you at the times you chose.

At each designated check-in, write down the time, where you are, what you're doing, and with whom you're doing it. For example, "It's 9 am on Tuesday and I'm writing a status report at Starbucks." Or, "It's 2:15 pm on Friday and I'm picking the kids up from school."

Ask yourself the following questions and note the responses in your journal:

- What am I doing?
- How am I feeling?

- Are my behaviors driven by positive beliefs about my future?
- Are my actions contributing to both my short-term and long-term goals?
- Are there other/better ways to accomplish what I'm doing?
- Rate yourself 1-10 on how hopeful you feel, with 1 being the least and 10 being the most.

At the end of the week, read through your journal. Look for the connections—or lack thereof—between beliefs and behaviors. Are you truly doing what's important? Are your immediate actions serving your vision of the future? In other words, is writing the report a worthwhile work endeavor, even if it's difficult? Is picking up your kids at school part of your overall vision for the kind of parent you wish to be?

Not that every moment of every day has to be spent in monumental undertakings—you do deserve relaxation and downtime. But by consciously tying beliefs to behaviors, and periodically checking in on yourself, you'll begin to focus on what's most important for realizing your vision of the future.

HOPEFUL HABITS

KEY TAKEAWAY #2

Though hope has been the subject of scores of poems, myths, and religious texts, the scientific study of hope, or *hope theory*, dates back less than a quarter-century. With Dr. Snyder's creation of the Hope Scale, levels of hopefulness can be measured by empirical means.

While Snyder, with his foundation in positive psychology, defines hope as the combination of goals, agency, and pathways, oncologist Dr. Jerome Groopman looks at hope through a physiological lens, tying belief to behavior to arrive at a desired result.

HOPEFUL BELIEF #2

Think of a past accomplishment of yours. It can be something dating as far back as childhood—like getting a blue ribbon in a swim meet—or it can be something recent, like writing your first guest blog for a colleague's website. What was the belief behind this accomplishment? Did the idea of winning inspire you to take on the hard work of regular swim practices? What about writing the guest blog? Is it part of a larger vision of creating your own platform? Of becoming a writer?

HOPEFUL BEHAVIOR #2

Identify the belief that drove your behavior toward the positive outcome you experienced. Did you win a blue ribbon because you enjoy athletics, like being part of a team, or love the feeling of winning? It could, of course, be all of these things, but see if you can pinpoint the primary underlying belief that got you into action. If you said, "competition," how can you apply your competitive spirit to another goal? To several goals? Try to muster that fabulous feeling you had of winning that swim meet as you tackle your next goal.

In chapter three, we'll look at how hope affects company culture, including commitment, change, and productivity.

CHAPTER 3

CREATING THE HOPE-DRIVEN CULTURE

Leading through Change, Challenge, and Chaos

"There is no medicine like hope, no incentive so great, and no tonic so powerful as expectation of something tomorrow."
—*Orison Swett Marden*

No doubt you've heard the term *servant leadership* buzzing around your workplace. While the concept likely started as far back as 500 BC with Chinese philosopher Lao-Tzu, others have popularized the notion in more recent times. Businessman Robert Greenleaf started the modern servant leadership movement in 1970 with his seminal essay, which suggested that leaders should put others' needs before their own quest for power or material gain. Pretty radical, right?

I find myself constantly explaining that servant leadership is not only the *right* thing to do, but it's also the *smart* thing to do. In my seventeen years as an executive coach and leadership consultant, I've discovered how rare—and precious—it is to meet leaders who are as dedicated to their individual workers as they are to the organization or their own success. It is these leaders—the *servant* leaders—who are the shapers of the hope-driven culture. When we treat our team members with trust, respect, and compassion— in other words, like most of us want to be treated—that positive experience is often passed along directly to the end user. Zappos, Southwest Airlines, and Ritz-Carlton are famous for taking care of staff the way they want them to take care of their customers. And it works.

But one leadership team blew me away with their commitment and creativity when it comes to servant leadership. I recently conducted a day-long strategy session with the Central Plains Sales Team for Abbott, a global medical device company. Abbott had acquired St. Jude Medical just months before, and VP of Sales Gray Fleming and his team had been absorbed in the acquisition. If you've ever gone through a corporate merger or buyout, you know how unnerving it can be, wondering how the changes will affect you.

Despite any uncertainty they might personally have been feeling, from our very first conversation, I could sense how dedicated and driven this team was. Gray and his entire senior sales team were on the phone for every one of our calls in preparation for the interactive seminar. They were determined to make the day meaningful and memorable—

and so was I. As Gray told me, "In our organization, we try to make servant leadership as straightforward as possible: lead from the back and remember to say thank you. When the opportunity was realized that we could *actually* serve our teams, it was a no-brainer, as there is no better way to demonstrate that thank you. In my opinion, the easiest way to find these opportunities is to focus on your 'role' in leadership versus your 'title' in the corporation."

The event was a great success, with lively participation, free-flowing ideas, and solid next-step action plans. But it was what happened *after* the workshop that really drove home the concept of servant leadership. Gray and his senior team, comprised of Dan Stephens, Charlie Robins, Brent Temple, and Gail Carlock, planned a surprise awards banquet dinner cruise around Lake Michigan.

As the group of nearly one hundred sales representatives walked up the gangplank and boarded the boat, they were greeted by the guys—*their own supervisors*—in waiters' uniforms bearing trays of wine and champagne. And it wasn't just for show. Gray and his leadership team waited on their team for the entire cocktail hour and on into dinner. But it didn't stop there: after handing out beautiful crystal awards and bottles of Veuve Clicquot in recognition of the year's sales superstars, the gentlemen invited award winners to sign their waiters' jackets with markers. A wearable wall of good wishes for future success.

While a group of leaders *literally* serving their own staffs was the cleverest demonstration of servant leadership I'd ever seen, there are plenty of things you can do sans champagne or waiters' jackets. See which of these expressions of servant leadership would feed your folks.

- *Recognize excellence.* In between the big awards functions and formal recognition events, remember to cite people who've exceeded expectations. Celebrate even the small wins with flowers, books, or $5 Starbucks cards. Send a personal thank you email, copying the entire team for a job well done. Or do something really special, like Graham Weston, one of the founders of web hosting company Rackspace, who used to give not only his parking space but also the use of his personal vehicle to a standout employee every month.

- *Offer ongoing education.* Nothing says, "I value you," more than investing in someone's growth and development. When time and budget allow, identify staff members to send to conferences, stipulating that they share takeaways with the rest of the team upon their return. Help people chart out their career paths, offering skills training and support to get them to the next level. Remember that life-long learners are the new gold standard for top talent.

- *Nurture your network.* Make sure you're giving back to the people who helped you get where you are today. Along with current employees who've had your back, reach out to former bosses, teachers, and coaches who have invested time and energy toward your success. A hand-written card, a friendly phone call, or a lunch invitation are easy ways to acknowledge that others have served you. After I gave a young staff member his first contract and encouraged him to buy the house he was considering, he called me every year for more than a decade on the anniversary of his closing date. Twenty years later, we're still buddies.

- *Hold informal outings.* While the company holiday party or annual retreat are great occasions to have on the calendar, don't overlook the opportunity for more casual connections. Gather everyone for a Friday afternoon happy hour or invite them to your house for a backyard barbecue. Like Gray and his gang, wait on them hand and foot and they'll know you really mean it when you talk about service.

- *Remember the small niceties.* Finally, just like your mother told you when you were a kid—and Gray reiterated—a simple please and thank you goes a long way. (Especially in email, where tone is notoriously absent.) As James Taylor sang in a song that probably wasn't about the workplace, but, perhaps, should have been, "Shower the people you love with love."

MANAGING CHANGE, CHALLENGE, AND CHAOS

Whether you choose to embrace it or ignore it, you can see the evidence of change all around you. Nowhere do we feel it more acutely than in the workplace. In fact, the world of work is changing so rapidly that many of today's jobs won't exist in a decade and many of the next decade's jobs don't exist today.[1] But it's not just our professional lives that leave us reeling from change. After all, who would have thought just a few years ago that they'd routinely climb into a total stranger's Prius or Civic to travel to the airport? Yet Uber clocks approximately forty million rides per month. From driverless cars to internet grocery shopping to artificial intelligence, the velocity and complexity of change are more challenging than ever.

If the enormity of these workplace changes leaves you reeling, you're not alone. But there's hope for the leaders of tomorrow. By creating a hope-driven culture, you'll be better able to overcome resistance and implement change in your team, division, or organization. And most importantly, in yourself. Before we get into methods to create a culture based on hope, let's look at three workplace trends that you need to understand if you want to succeed in an increasingly complex and change-driven marketplace.

THE CHAOS NORM

The very nature of workplace change has, well, *changed*. While there has always been an ebb and flow, organizational change today is constant, relentless, and continually accelerating. The sheer pace of change, let alone the volume, is dizzying. Employees often feel as though they've finally found a client

---

1   Andrew Heikkila, "Jobs That Don't Exist Yet: How to Prepare for the Future of Work," *Business 2 Community*, March 16, 2016, http://www.business2community.com/human-resources/jobs-dont-exist-yet-prepare-future-work-01484828#ftRw3sSokdWymkeS.97.

solution that works or implemented a process improvement, only to be hit by the next wave. And they're right.

That's the new *chaos norm*, where heightened competition, increasingly sophisticated (and demanding) consumers, and rapid advances in technology drive the need for and the pace of change. One of the best ways to get comfortable with all that discomfort is to create an environment where people feel safe and accepted. Simple, but not easy.

In my book *You Unstuck: Mastering the New Rules of Risk-taking in Work and Life*, I detail what I call the *Immediate Negative Response* (or INR), the knee-jerk resistance to change that is based on our biological survival instinct to avoid danger and seek familiarity. But it is the leader's role not only to overcome his or her own fear-based feelings, but also to ensure that employees recognize that while change can be anxiety provoking, every new obstacle is an opportunity to learn and improve.

FUNCTION FLUIDITY

Leaders and managers, especially those with hiring power, have long thought about employees in terms of track record. Not necessarily a bad way to judge, past behavior is often the best indication of future behavior. But tomorrow's leaders must begin to look at employees in terms of potential. Soon workers will be in a state of constant training as they are assigned to teams and projects based on their ability to learn, grow, problem solve, and lead others. Tasks will be assigned based on what a professional *can* do rather than what they *have* done. And workers who embrace, rather than tolerate, new challenges will be the corporate rock stars of tomorrow.

CORPORATION AS COMMUNITY

Paradoxically, as changes are implemented more and more swiftly, leaders will need to loosen their hold on the workforce. Through transparency of mission and constant communication, effective future leaders will foster trust and collaboration, encouraging coworkers to create deep and meaningful relationships, even fast friendships. With the right mindset, these relationships can flourish in shared physical space or through virtual means, as improved technical connectivity continues to place us face-to-face, whether from across the hall or across the globe.

With flextime policies (and changing attitudes about people using them without penalty), global teams, and 24/7 accountability, future leaders will need to create avenues for engagement, replacing bureaucracy with flexibility and hierarchy with collaboration. Engagement tools such as intranet portals, company-supported volunteer activities, and free-flowing information will turn the workplace into an environment where employees *want* to be, rather than *have* to be. In a later chapter, we'll see how these trends are expected to affect generational groups from Millennials to Traditionalists.

CREATING THE HOPE-DRIVEN CULTURE

So what does all this mean for established and emerging leaders, particularly those in the areas of rapid change and growth, who must purposefully blend the best practices of people management with advances in processes if they wish to keep up, or better yet, stay ahead? What do they need to understand about helping employees navigate uncertainty and ambiguity? And what qualities do leaders (or future leaders) need to develop in themselves to facilitate lasting change?

In a Gallup poll of more than ten thousand workplace participants, the four traits cited most often as what followers wanted from their leaders were compassion, stability, trust, and hope. Needless to say, absent those leadership qualities, as is often the case in the midst of reorganization and ongoing change, employees are often not at their most engaged or productive. When Gallup asked workers if their managers and leaders made them feel hopeful about the future, among those who said yes, 69% also scored high on a scale of engagement in their work. Of those who said their managers did not instill a sense of hopefulness about their futures, only 1% scored high on the engagement measure.

In my ongoing research on hope in the workplace as I coach and consult around the world, I see a clear pattern emerging, highlighted by the following:

- *Most* professionals see hope as an essential element of leadership
- *Some* professionals feel that they intentionally feed hope in their workplace
- *Few* professionals believe that their organizations inspire hopefulness among their employees

The disconnect is all too obvious. While many workers see the relevance of hope—especially when defined as positive beliefs driving positive behaviors—they're not sure how to spread hope within the employee base. And they certainly don't believe that their organization's leadership is doing a good job inspiring it in any overall sense. So how can you become an agent of change and close the hope gap? For me, it all starts with communication. No surprise, perhaps, since my entire professional background has been focused, either directly or indirectly, on effective communication and the use of language as a workforce motivator. At no time was this more apparent to me than when I was recruited to head media relations and corporate communications for the worldwide television group at Universal Studios. I joined the studio shortly after it had been purchased by Seagram, the spirits company. A massive reorganization was underway, and in a span of approximately two years, every business unit—music, motion pictures, theme parks, television, and consumer products—had new management in place.

That was a lot of change for people who had previously worked for the longest-running leadership team in Hollywood history. The divisions had been famously siloed, and the reporting lines often had more to do with historic relationships—from friendships to fallings out— than logic. At my first staff meeting where I centralized the communication functions from five different areas, I discovered a number of my direct reports had worked at the studio for twenty-plus years, and yet had never met their counterparts, sometimes working just a building or two away. I was astounded that they had not gotten together for a cup of coffee, out of curiosity at least, if not to share strategies and resources.

But it was when I tried to network outside of my department that I truly hit the brick wall of hopelessness. Throughout the organization, people were used to keeping their heads down, doing their jobs, and protecting their turf. I had an uphill fight just to get acquainted with my new colleagues. Undeterred, I got in my golf cart—the optimal mode of transportation on the massive Universal back lot—and went out to introduce myself to producers, directors, HR staff, costume designers, and finance executives. I wanted to talk to anyone who had a stake in the success of the television group and was willing to spend a few minutes with me. What I discovered was a workforce in the throes of transformation fatigue: tired of all the management changes, unclear about the future direction of the company, and fearful for the stability of their jobs.

But I also found that, with a bit of encouragement, most people were willing to reignite that spark of hope in the form of engagement and collaboration. They wanted to be on a winning team, even if there were all new players on the field. Once a relationship was established with my studio colleagues, trust and respect weren't far behind. For example, it wasn't long before my team and I were able to persuade our theme park counterparts, with their built-in audience of entertainment aficionados, to float a five-story banner from the top of the *Jurassic Park* ride to promote the premiere of a television series. Or to host a swag-filled TV night for the Universal Studios tour guides so we could update them with fun factoids about our shows, tidbits of knowledge they could pass along to the captive fans on the tram tour, thus increasing audience viewership and loyalty.

With some shared success behind us, it was far easier to chart a mutually beneficial course into the future.

The critical need to foster trust and create a shared plan for the future—what I understood instinctively in my early days of leadership, and what propelled me to solicit face-to-face meetings, even with less-than-enthusiastic participants—has been backed up by numerous research studies. According to Dr. Shane Lopez, business professor and author of *Making Hope Happen*, leaders must do three things in order to create a hope-fueled workplace:[2]

- Create and sustain excitement about the future
- Remove existing obstacles to goals and avoid creating new ones
- Re-establish goals whenever circumstances necessitate

Yet, even when we recognize the benefits of hopefully embracing change, most of us will go to great lengths to avoid shaking up our lives. Don't we all know someone who claims to be dissatisfied with her job, boss, or coworkers, yet never seems to do anything about it? Or a company that has gone through massive change management initiatives only to have employees backslide into old behaviors as soon as they experience the least bit of discomfort?

Understanding *why* people resist change is the first step in figuring out *how* to get them to change. Here are some of the common resistance scenarios I see in the workplace:

---

2   Shane J. Lopez, *Making Hope Happen: Create the Future You Want for Yourself and Others* (New York: Atria Paperback, 2013).

- **Biological hardwiring.** Change triggers our "fear center," the primitive area of our brain known as the amygdala. As part of our biological early warning system, fear puts us on high alert so we can fight or flee when faced with danger. But if we don't understand that our brains may perceive the unfamiliar as danger, our anxiety may cause us to back down from changes that are not only harmless, but actually beneficial. *We ask ourselves: why do I feel so stressed?*

- **Feeling out of control.** When faced with change, whether it takes the form of new people, systems, or technology, we often feel out of control. Everything we're used to is taken away—at least, that's what it feels like—and we're given a new set of expectations that requires us to shift our mindset and wade into a whole new reality. *We want to know: who needs all that ambiguity?*

- **Misplaced loyalty.** Changing our beliefs can make us feel as though we're leaving our trusted colleagues behind. When a new process is put in place or a new manager brings a different perspective, it can make us feel (even unconsciously) that we have to abandon the people or training we relied on in the past. *We wonder: was my old boss really that bad?*

- **Fear of failure.** Some people fear that a changed workplace may mean they're no longer relevant, that they've suddenly become part of the old guard and may not cut it in this brave new world. Employees often feel challenged or that they might not have the proper skills or attitude to embrace the culture shift. *We worry: am I really up to the challenge?*

- **Old habits die hard.** Most of us love our same old, same old routines. We want to cling to the comfort of familiarity and may need some convincing that all this change actually adds up to improvement and is not just change for change's sake. *We whine: isn't the world complex enough already?*

But when leaders take the time and effort to clarify the benefits of change—explaining clearly why the change is needed and how things will be better once the change is implemented—they'll begin to rally support. Roll out your change initiative throughout the company with a communication program customized for your culture. Involve people at all levels of the organization, including the "naysayers," who may have contrarian but nonetheless productive solutions.

Take consistent action, using strategic triggers, including visual reminders, accountability buddies, and touch-base meetings, to stay on track. Above all, be realistic about timeframes and remember that change takes place over time, not overnight. If you drop the ball (which you will), pick it up and get rolling again right away.

EDMUNDS: A CULTURE POWERED BY TRUST

Who would have thought that a paperback car guide from the 1960s would grow into an online resource for car buyers from all over the country? Today, car shoppers turn to Edmunds.com for information and data to aid in their car-buying experience. I got to know Edmunds a couple of years ago when I was buying a new car, and coincidentally, soon after, I had the opportunity to work with their employee experience team on several projects.

Edmunds, with their auto-themed headquarters, has an array of cool perks that help define not only their physical space but also their culture, including a 1948 Cadillac Fleetwood repurposed into a beer and coffee bar (the beer taps are inside the Cadillac), a game room featuring an array of classic video games, 130 feet of sliding glass panels that transform the office into an indoor/outdoor workspace, and a thirty-two-foot custom stainless steel slide that connects their two floors. But what really defines their culture is their concept of TRUST—that is, togetherness, resourcefulness, urgency, simplicity, and transparency.

As Executive Director of Employment Experience Jamie Epstein told me, "What blew me away when I joined Edmunds was the focus on creating a culture that enables employees to do their best work. We make decisions by asking ourselves if what we're doing will benefit *both* the business and the culture." Key to Edmunds' hopeful culture is the ongoing communication about the future, for both the company and the individual. In a program called Fuel Your Potential (no surprise, they love using automotive terms), everyone who manages direct reports helps each team member come up with a stretch project that will aid in their professional development while it adds value to the company. The conversations around these stretch projects go from top to bottom throughout the entire organization in what Edmunds calls their Cascade Development process. As part of the process, employees are routinely asked what kind of projects they want to work on next, how they want to build skills and expertise, and what they want for their future career path.

Citing their commitment to transparency, Jamie adds, "We create great excitement about the future by clarifying goals for the year, sharing them with everyone, and then keeping the conversation alive." Edmunds president Seth Berkowitz sends regular email blasts describing company strategy, conversations with fellow employees, and even his own development plans. CEO Avi Steinlauf hosts the entire company of nearly 700 employees for lunch in the Great Room once a week for what's called the "Cadillac Catch-up." He updates the team on current developments and events, but more than that, provides an opportunity to introduce new hires and congratulate employees on work anniversaries, babies, and other major milestones in their personal and professional lives.

"It brings people together," Jamie says. "We leave the meeting knowing who the new employees are and who's had exciting personal developments. It really makes us feel connected to one another." Looks like togetherness is a good way to manage change and build culture.

THE INDIVIDUAL INFLUENCER

Although Edmunds is dedicated to togetherness, many workplace culture changes start with the individual influencers who have the commitment, credibility, and communications skills to instill these concepts within a broader swath of the organization. Julia Beck, workplace innovator and founder of the It's Working Project, which is dedicated to getting new parents back to work, says it sometimes takes only one person to instigate meaningful change.

She calls this person *Employee Zero* (like the Patient Zero at the front end of a contagion), but cautions that not just anybody can be a change agent. Being a successful change agent requires that an individual put his or her neck on the line *or* find someone who is willing to step up and use their influence to support that individual.[3] Either way, change makers should be prepared to make a compelling case for the change they're seeking by trying some or all of the following.

1. **Articulate the desired change.** Complaining that a rule needs to be repealed or a behavior needs to be stopped is rarely enough. Instead, influencers must be ready to paint a vivid picture of the change they're seeking. A few years ago, I presented a keynote and emceed a panel at Kellogg's first-ever national women's leadership event. Although the company had a number of regional events for female employees, one innovative executive, the *Employee Zero*, recognized the need to bring all these disparate groups together and took it upon herself to organize the

---

3   Robin Camarote, "How to Make Powerful Changes at Work by Being 'Employee Zero,'" *Inc.*, July 27, 2016, https://www.inc.com/robin-camarote/how-to-make-powerful-changes-at-work-by-being-employee-zero.html.

event. Her passion got the attention of a senior HR executive, the *Employee Zero Supporter,* who backed her plan, and a new women's leadership forum was born.

2. **Find others who feel the same way.** If you've discovered an area ripe for meaningful change, chances are other people have noticed the same thing, even if they haven't spoken up about it. Bring them into the fold. The more employees you can include in your change initiative, the more compelling it will be to management. By demonstrating that lots of people, rather than just a few individuals, will be positively impacted by the change, you've got a much stronger case. When it comes to change, there really is strength in numbers.

3. **Prepare for pushback.** Change is rarely embraced easily or at the first suggestion. Be prepared by thinking through all the objections you might receive, whether legitimate business concerns or lame excuses, and be ready to counter each one. If you fail the first time, regroup and try again. Your executive committee may be recalcitrant, but if it's important, persist.

LANGUAGE OF THE HOPEFUL LEADER

There's an old joke: "If you're leading and nobody's following, maybe you're just taking a walk." Not so funny, perhaps, if you're the one attempting to create some followership. I've found that creating specific leadership language that is authentic to your style and culture can go a long way to creating an engaged following and collaborative culture within the organization.

The challenge for leadership is clear. Managers must come to know their team members' strengths and weaknesses on a deeper level than ever before, recognizing and rewarding traits such as flexibility, strategic thinking, and creativity. Professionals with a mindset for life-long learning will be the new currency. For some leaders as well as their employees, this will be incredibly frustrating. For others, it will be an exhilarating invitation to master new skills and take on new functions as needed.

While many leaders are excellent strategists whose technical abilities have gotten them to a senior level, they must learn to give the same level of attention and care when it comes to communication. Here are some strategies for incorporating simple and straightforward leadership language into your everyday vocabulary.

"This is the vision."

As a leader, you want to share your perspective on the competitive landscape of your industry with your team as often as possible. Yes, you're dealing with some proprietary and confidential matters that can't be discussed, but strive for transparency and inclusion in your communication. When you're an open book, people rightly feel that you have nothing to hide, that you trust them enough to confide in them, and that you want them on your team.

"Here's the plan."

Because you're still the boss of the organization, division, or project team—despite the increasingly popular "we don't have titles, we're all equals here" mentality—people expect you to step up and have a plan. Look one year ahead and start working backwards, quarter by quarter, month by month, week by week. What are the results you're looking for? Be clear and concise about anticipated outcomes—and don't overlook the obvious. Not everyone knows what you know.

Set your high-level objectives, critical tasks, milestone markers, and project ownership. Avoid ambiguity and corporate speak—everything needs to be crystal clear to everyone on the team. Let your team or task leaders concern themselves with the details of the process and how to meet expectations while you stay focused on high-value activities. Most of all, remember to keep it simple!

"What do you need from me?"

Check in regularly—at least as often as the milestone markers you've established—to make sure everyone is on task and on time. Know what your people do well and tap into their talents. Find out what each team member needs, directly or through your managers if you're in a large organization, to get the job done effectively. Resolve conflicts quickly and give feedback frequently. Blend kindness with candor but don't waste time sugarcoating reactions or pussyfooting around problems. Not only will you make things worse, you'll teach others to follow your conflict-avoiding behavior.

"How can we improve?"

Keep a "we're good, but we can always be better" attitude and encourage everyone to regularly contribute strategies and suggestions to improve the workplace. Take a page directly from *kaizen* (literally meaning "change for the good"), the Japanese auto manufacturers' practice of encouraging workers at all levels to offer ideas for increased quality and productivity, and you'll make ongoing people improvement part of your organizational DNA.

While you may be doing fine right now, if you aren't making ongoing enhancements to communication, it won't be long until your competitors out-innovate you. As a leader, you need to get out, ask questions, and solicit creative ideas from people at every level of the company so that continuous improvement is a team sport and not a competition.

"Woohoo. Let's celebrate!"

Celebrate success along the way. Not just the big scores, but also the small wins, including meeting your milestones. Institutionalize celebrations that fit your unique culture. A great example is the Sacred Boomerang Award that innovative design firm Kahler Slater uses to welcome back former employees who've returned to the company after time away. Or the FANATI Award, given to a partner business by web hosting company Rackspace for "fanatical" customer service. Even a good old Friday afternoon beer bash just for the heck of it can increase collaboration and camaraderie.

ARE YOU READY TO LEAD?

As we've seen with the individual influencers, everyone can play a part in the positive development of their company's culture—even those in an early career stage. I worked briefly with an extremely bright young woman named Jessica. A Millennial at the older end of the scale, she'd gotten her MBA and had been in the workforce for a couple of years when we first met. She hired me for some short-term coaching after she landed what she considered her first "big" job at a global consulting firm. Jessica knew she had a lot to learn in her new role, where she would be helping clients implement new structures and strategies, but she was determined to put herself on the fast-track to management.

At the time we started our coaching, she was straddling two teams, providing support to a team in charge of technical accounts as well as working with a team in charge of financial strategy. She wasn't sure what her future would be at the company, but had the good sense to realize that her fate (and brand) was in her hands, and that it was up to her to decide how to shape it.

The first thing I advised her to do was to take the time to contemplate, fantasize, meditate—whatever you want to call it—about what her ideal life would look like in ten years. Pretty obvious, and yet, after seventeen years as a coach, I can probably count on one hand the number of people who actually take the time and effort to visualize their own future. If they did, we'd have a lot more than 28% of Americans actively saving for retirement, right?[4]

---

4   Elyssa Kirkham, "1 in 3 Americans Has Saved $0 for Retirement,"

It didn't take Jessica long to create a clear picture of what success looked like to her. She wanted to be in senior leadership within her industry, though not necessarily at the same company. She wanted to work on financial strategy accounts—the bigger the better. And she wanted to make an above-average income so she and her husband could raise a family and have a good quality of life in their new home in New York City, not an inexpensive place to live.

With her newfound future focus firmly in mind, Jessica decided that being on the strategy team was going to move her into management much faster than staying on the tech side, where she didn't feel she had either the training or the interest. Not that she couldn't coast along, learning new skills and contributing solid work, but why should she? She was ready to shine. But as a new employee, she also didn't want to burn any bridges with her colleagues or appear to be one of those ship-jumping Millennials so many managers complain about.

Her two main goals were 1) getting to know as many people within the company as she could to build advocates and allies and 2) getting off the tech team and onto the strategy team without appearing ungrateful. Naturally, neither of those would mean anything if she didn't continue to deliver value to the organization. But over-delivering was in Jessica's DNA. She couldn't *not* deliver.

When I asked her the quickest way to meet her new colleagues, including senior leaders and subordinates, she came up with a simple but brilliant idea that fit her personal style as well as the company's culture. As part of a young, aggressive organization, Jessica and her coworkers played almost as hard as they worked. So Jessica hatched a plan to take on the task of managing the basketball brackets for the March Madness season, which no one at the company had ever done. She was a diehard college sports fan (though her University of Illinois home team rarely made the finals), so her desire to take on the project was as authentic as it was pragmatic.

After being cited by her division head at an all-hands meeting for creating a fun bonding experience in which everyone could participate, Jessica felt like she was on the map. She'd been able to interact with people who might otherwise have taken months to get to know—all in the name of fun, friendship, and company culture. It didn't take long for the conversations to happen about where she wanted to go within the organization. In less than three months, she was a full-time member of the strategy team, and in less than a year, she was offered a much bigger position at a competitor company. All because she had a future-focused vision and the guts to take action toward it.

At the opposite end of the spectrum, Carlos was a young man a few years into his entertainment career whom a former colleague had asked me to mentor. A creative and likeable guy who was a new manager handling promotions and events for an independent film studio, Carlos's responsibility was to put his company on the map through premiere parties and film festival events. He was a smart guy, but rather than rising up the ranks of corporate entertainment as he longed to do, he'd been stuck at the same level for several years.

When I asked him point-blank what was stopping him from asking for a promotion or changing companies, he had a list of excuses about why he wasn't ready or qualified, and why no one took him seriously. When I gently suggested that perhaps he didn't take himself seriously, he backpedaled and said his job wasn't "all that bad." A few months later, I heard Carlos had been laid off. I was sorry for him, but not surprised. Why was it that Jessica got the memo about beliefs driving behavior while Carlos did not?

Again, that's what this book is about: belief driving behavior based on the science of *hope theory*. Hope theory is not about sugarcoating reality or turning lemons into lemonade. Rather, it's a willingness to staunchly move forward even in the face of difficult or desperate circumstances. And best of all, it's learnable.

LEADING AT WORK, LEADING IN LIFE

So why is it that people with roughly the same level of expertise, education, and opportunity like Carlos and Jessica can have such different approaches to managing their lives? To stepping into leadership positions, whether they work for a small business or a Fortune 500 company? We'll look at some of the stories we tell ourselves about what we're capable of in an upcoming chapter. Right now, let's look at who wants to lead and who doesn't. The research might surprise you.

First of all, not everyone wants a leadership position, no matter how hard they try to convince themselves that that's what they are "supposed" to want. A nationwide

CareerBuilder poll, conducted by Harris in 2014, found that among the nearly four thousand workers surveyed, only 34% aspired to leadership positions and, among those, only 7% wanted C-level roles. The poll results revealed that while 40% of men aimed for leadership positions, only 29% of women desired the top spots. Interestingly, 39% of African Americans and 44% of LGBT workers aspired to key leadership roles.

As for the other 66% who are apparently happy to stay right where they are or keep their professional aspirations modest, Rosemary Haefner, vice president of human resources at CareerBuilder, said, "Upon entering the prime of their careers, workers who haven't yet ascended to a leadership role often decide, for a variety of reasons, that their career is fine right where it is. And that's okay, because every organization needs skilled workers who excel at specific functions just as much as they need leaders to guide them."[5]

Fair enough, we don't all have to want to be top dogs at work. But what about the rest of your life? Even if you are legitimately happy with your current professional role, don't you want more *personally* for yourself and your loved ones? Assuming you chose this book (or it chose you) for a reason, I'm betting you want to be a leader in your own life, as well as that of your family, school, place of worship, or community. Read on to start forming those hopeful habits now.

---

5 Nicole Torres, "Most People Don't Want to Be Managers," *Harvard Business Review*, September 18, 2014, https://hbr.org/2014/09/most-people-dont-want-to-be-managers.

HOPEFUL HABITS

KEY TAKEAWAY #3

As the workplace changes with unprecedented speed and complexity, it is critical for emerging and established leaders to recognize what tomorrow's workplace will look like, so they can begin to prepare today. By consciously linking beliefs to workplace behaviors, you'll be much more likely to speed up your growth curve.

HOPEFUL BELIEF #3

Think about a change you'd like to make at your workplace. It should be specific, measurable, and significant or it's unlikely you—and others—will want to stick with it. Like the executive who used her influence to start a national women's leadership initiative at Kellogg's. Or Jessica, who turned March Madness into a networking opportunity.

Next, think about yourself as *Employee Zero*. Do you have the influence to make this change happen on your own? Or do you need someone with more clout to champion your idea? If so, who would that be? How will you describe the desired change to your leadership or to your *Employee Zero Supporter*?

HOPEFUL BEHAVIOR #3

Now, take the first step. Write out your change story. What problem would it solve? Who would benefit? How difficult would it be to initiate? How would you communicate the change and how will you make it stick? What obstacles or pushback can you expect?

Once you've gotten your story as fine-tuned as possible, go pitch it directly to management as *Employee Zero*, or sell it to a potential *Employee Zero Supporter* who can get on board and help you make it happen.

CHAPTER 4

LEADING HIGH-PASSION, HIGH-PERFORMANCE TEAMS

The Secret Ingredient You Need for Success

"Talent wins games, but teamwork wins championships."
—Michael Jordan

In a recent *New York Times* article, Julia Rozovsky, now a people analytics manager at Google, described the study group to which she was assigned when she was earning her MBA at Yale. A common practice in business school, being part of a study group is meant to enhance the academic experience while giving grad students the opportunity to become adept at navigating teams, which is likely to become a large part of their future work life. Julia's team members seemed to have a lot in common: they were all smart and hardworking, had gone to similar schools for their undergrad degrees, and several had worked in comparable organizations. Nonetheless, Julia discovered a level of credit grabbing and jockeying for position that made her personally uncomfortable and the group itself unproductive.[1]

While Julia was looking for another team to join, a classmate suggested that she try a "case competition team," where groups solved problems with real-world solutions for cash and prizes. The goal and format were different, but the teamwork still entailed research, financial and business analysis, report writing, and presentations. Although these team members couldn't have been more diverse—an army officer, a researcher, a healthcare professional, and a consultant to a refugee program—they gelled immediately.

While Julia liked the study group members from the first team one-on-one, she found them very challenging when they came together as a unit. Conversely, while she loved being part of the case competition team, she actually had far less in common with those team members. Though it may not have been part of the curriculum, what Julia likely learned from both of these experiences was that serving on teams could be exhilarating or challenging depending less on the skills of the members than on their personalities. Welcome to the truth about teams.

---

1   Charles Duhigg, "What Google Learned From Its Quest to Build the Perfect Team," *The New York Times Magazine*, February 25, 2016, https://www.nytimes.com/2016/02/28/magazine/what-google-learned-from-its-quest-to-build-the-perfect-team.html?_r=0.

THE PERSONALITY OF HIGH-PERFORMANCE TEAMS

Teams are a way of life in the corporate world, in our schools and communities, and in the dynamic of families. All the way back to hunter-gatherer days, it was essential that people learned to work together to feed their tribes and fight their enemies. While the focus of teams has shifted through the centuries, they are still one of our most crucial social structures. How we introduce hopefulness into our teams can be the difference between joyful collaboration and frustrating second-guessing. In this chapter, we'll look at what makes an effective team.

As I grew as a leader, recruiting and developing communications teams at Turner Broadcasting and Universal after I left Sony, I came to see that, often, the more heterogeneous the group, the more successful the project outcome. While it was my job as a leader to build a foundation of hope, trust, and respect, it was also critical to bring together the best combination of contributors. The right personalities, along with the right mix of skills, could help teams operate at a level greater than the sum of its parts. But when the personalities didn't mesh, it could be disastrous, with lack of engagement, failure to make shared decisions, or worse, overt infighting.

While you may not always have the luxury of hand-picking your team members (as they may sign up for, or be assigned to, your team), the more you understand the personalities involved, the more you'll be able to predict and manage the group dynamic. In other words, the more effectively you'll be able to lead your team. See if you recognize yourself and your coworkers in the list of team member archetypes below.

1. ***The Driver.*** Drivers are the leaders who keep the team focused and moving forward. Often, these are designated leaders, but in flat teams or organizations where everyone is meant to be equal, leaders often emerge naturally. If there's no clear leader, one of the first team tasks should be to choose someone to direct the team. Typically, that person will be charged with guiding group discussions, assigning roles, and managing conflict—in short, keeping the team moving efficiently toward the end goal. ***Drivers: focused, outcome oriented, communicative, opinionated***

2. ***The Organizer.*** With a strong Organizer on board, the team leader may be able to shift some of the administrative activities. Organizers are process oriented and often adept with lists, calendars, and charts. Rather than impose their will on others (as some Drivers tend to do), they love to put systems in place to create an atmosphere of order and harmony where everyone can thrive. Be grateful if you have someone like a former assistant of mine who told me proudly at our initial interview, "I live to organize." It was music to my Driver ears and the beginning of a long and fruitful relationship.

Organizers: process oriented, detailed, supportive, team focused

3. *The Visionary.* Visionaries are the creative engines of the team machine. Though they may sometimes seem lost in the clouds, it is precisely their ability to dream—and dream big—that can bring a breakthrough idea to the team. These creative types aren't just found in positions like marketing or design, but can be found in any area. Learn to tolerate their flights of fancy, give them encouragement to express their thoughts, and you may find they're full of fresh process and people solutions that can help solve even the thorniest problems. *Visionaries: creative, big picture, imaginative, future focused*

4. *The Naysayer.* Contrarians of the corporate world have gotten a bad rap for being negative. But that's actually their blessing. If you can put up with the Naysayers' occasional sourpuss style, you'll discover that their out-of-the-box way of looking at the world can bring an enormous amount of innovation to the group. Deal with their disruptive attitudes, listen to their wild ideas, embrace their sometimes-unusual methods, and you may strike gold. *Naysayers: disruptive, innovative, challenging, idea people*

5. *The Diplomat.* Like the Organizer, the Diplomat is focused on the common good. Diplomats are relationship builders and talented

team players who can soothe ruffled feathers and bring out the best in others. They may not always like to take the lead, but they'll happily weigh in with their own thoughts and encourage input from others. Respect their emotional nature, appreciate their calm demeanor, and you'll have a connector who can rally the team even in the most difficult moments. *Diplomats: relationship oriented, conflict resolvers, harmonious, influential*

6. *The Expert.* Though everyone on the team should have skills that allow them to contribute to problem solving and organizational growth (except for the Wild Card), there should be at least one person on the team with deep subject-matter knowledge. The Expert is the go-to answer person on the problem at hand, a skilled researcher, and someone who can pose and answer the questions no one else even thought to ask. Treasure them. *Experts: knowledgeable, research-savvy, informed, problem solver*

7. *The Wild Card.* Not every team needs a Wild Card, that is, a person who comes from a completely different discipline and might not normally interact with the group. But by bringing a Wild Card onto a team or even just an occasional meeting, particularly brainstorming sessions where all ideas are welcome, you may get some great surprises. People who are new to the organization or business unit can often be great Wild Cards, bringing fresh perspectives and

competitive knowledge that can be invaluable. *Wild Cards: fresh thinkers, challenging, information seekers, creative*

Ideally, by having a mix of personalities, you get the benefit of different skills sets, depth and type of experience, and temperaments. One way to break the ice with a new team kickoff is to identify personality types and discuss how the group might click or clash. By putting differences on the table for discussion, you not only build trust and rapport, but you make being "other" a positive benefit to the entire team, instead of an isolating factor.

MORE PERSONALITY PROFILES

If you want some additional help identifying the personality types of your group members, there are a number of free and low-cost assessments on the market. Try one or two of these tests with your team to get more insights on individual performance styles and how best to work together collaboratively. Check out the following and see what suits your vibe and budget:

- The *Myers-Briggs Type Indicator®* (MBTI®) was created to help people understand their psychological preferences and decision-making style. It's based on Carl Jung's conclusions about four distinct methods for how people perceive the world around them, including sensation, intuition, feeling, and thinking.

- The *DISC Profile* was designed to aid professionals in communication, teamwork, and productivity. By understanding your dominant and secondary DISC traits—which include Dominance, Influence, Steadiness, and Conscientiousness—you can build more effective teams, enhance your leadership style, and handle conflicts.

- The *Winslow Profile* is an online system that measures twenty-four aspects of the personality, behaviors, and attitudes of employees. It provides comprehensive feedback and specific prescriptive suggestions for enhancing performance for individuals and teams.

- The *Clifton StrengthsFinder* assessment identifies employees' top talents, allowing them to use their skills for optimal performance and increased engagement. Developed by Gallup executive Tom Rath, fans of this format appreciate that the profile guides users to build on strengths rather than focus on weaknesses.

- The *Color Code Personality Test* looks at not only *what* you do but *why* you do it, providing insights into how you and others around you tick. This test places people into four color categories that help show why we connect with some people and clash with others. The four Color Code types are Red (power and leadership), Blue (integrity and relationships), White (objective and tolerant), and Yellow (fun loving and social).

No doubt, members of both teams on which Julia served at Yale had strong skills. But the case competition team clearly had a mix of personalities that helped that group become greater than the sum of its individual players. With their easy camaraderie and collaboration, the case group was able to create a high-performing team, handily winning a competition by suggesting that an out-of-date campus snack bar be replaced with a micro-gym, which was installed on the Yale campus shortly after the contest.

FIVE FACTORS FOR EFFECTIVE TEAM COMMUNICATION

The importance of personalities notwithstanding, there's one factor that is by far the most critical determinant of team success: communication. While it may seem obvious that teams that communicate effectively are apt to be more successful than ones that don't, the data tells a far richer story than that. Under the direction of Alex "Sandy" Pentland at MIT's Human Dynamics Lab, researchers have conducted multiple studies on the intersection of human behavior and technology to look for patterns that can help improve organizations, public health, transportation, and financial systems.[2]

One of their most striking discoveries is that *how* teams communicate is far more critical in terms of productivity

---

2   Alex "Sandy" Pentland, "The New Science of Building Great Teams," *Harvard Business Review*, April 2012, https://hbr.org/2012/04/the-new-science-of-building-great-teams.

and success than *what* they communicate. Pentland and his group observed that they could feel a certain "buzz" in highly engaged groups, even if they had little understanding of the subject matter that was being discussed. While many social scientists and organizational experts had assumed that group dynamics were too intangible to quantify, Pentland and his team decided to investigate.

First, they identified similar types of teams in diverse industries across the globe, including healthcare and banking, that had experienced varying degrees of success. Next, the researchers gave each team member subject an electronic badge that could collect data on individual communication, including volume of voice, number of interactions, physical stance when communicating, and much more. After studying multiple groups, they came to the conclusion that three key factors affected communication and, ultimately, team success. Those factors are *energy, engagement,* and *exploration.*

Where we might think conventionally of *energy* as strength or vitality, Pentland's group defined it as the number and nature of shared communications, anything from a head nod to an affirmation to a conversation. What they determined—and what I've long since observed as a speaker—is that face-to-face communication is far more effective than any other form, with email and texting the least effective, and video chatting, particularly with a limited number of people, landing somewhere in the middle of the communication effectiveness spectrum. Teams with a high level of team energy would have numerous interactions, often delivered in face-to-face settings.

They dubbed the second factor in effective team communication *engagement,* describing it as the "distribution of energy" among teammates. In other words, it's where team members interact with all other team members with a similar level of frequency and enthusiasm, rather than, for example, focusing their communications solely on the leader or one or two other team members. Teams that had high levels of interaction equally dispersed among members were deemed highly engaged, while those with an inequity of talk time and connection were considered less engaged. This type of low engagement was seen frequently in groups that were geographically distant and whose most common mode of communication was by phone or email. Team success, they found, was far more likely in the highly engaged teams.

The final success factor in team communication is *exploration*, defined by Pentland's group as the practice of engaging with members outside the team. Individuals who sought connections and information outside their immediate circles, and then brought that information back to the group, expanded the knowledge base and problem-solving potential. While it is difficult to be highly engaged in your own group and also spend time with those outside the group, the data clearly showed that teams that found the balance between these two conflicting factors were by far the most successful.

Perhaps the most startling revelation of all is that knowledge and talent contribute far less to team success than we commonly think. But by understanding how individual personalities co-exist, and then training the teams to learn successful patterns of communication, you can greatly increase your odds for success.

What did the MIT team—themselves a mix of social scientists and data engineers—learn about what a successful team looks like? Here are five critical factors:

1. All team members talk and listen in approximately the same amounts, keeping their contributions succinct and straightforward.
2. Team members physically face each other, and their discussions and gestures are lively and energetic.
3. Members connect with one another, not just the team leader.
4. Members carry on side conversations or back-channel discussions within the team. (The old leadership advisory—"Let's just have one meeting, people"—doesn't really stand up to scrutiny.)
5. Members meet, break, go exploring outside the team, and bring back information to share with teammates.

Organizations, including a call center in the United States and a bank in the Czech Republic, that enacted changes based on this data, found that efficiencies and outcomes improved rapidly. By instigating simple solutions, like having an entire team take their coffee break at the same time, or replacing small cafeteria tables with longer community tables that encouraged interaction with strangers, companies increased engagement significantly, making the way for far greater team success. How might you implement some simple changes that encourage lively face-to-face interaction?

ESCAPE FROM MEETING HELL

Of course, once you've built an effective team, identified the personalities of its members, and learned some new communication techniques, you still have to bring your team together in one of the most maligned structures in the business world: *meetings*. One of the biggest complaints I hear from leaders, managers, and rank-and-file employees is the number of meetings they're expected to attend and how little actually gets accomplished at those meetings. According to the Bureau of Labor Statistics' Time Use Survey, American workers spend an average of 8.7 hours per week in meetings. And I know plenty of people who would argue that that number is way too low. If you've ever had to suffer through a prep meeting to plan for a meeting, attended the meeting itself, and then attended the follow-up meeting to assess the meeting you just had, you know what I'm talking about.

But meetings don't have to be a hopeless drain on your time and energy if you go about them in a thoughtful and disciplined way. Here are some tips for making your meetings more meaningful, productive, and, yes, even fun.

1. Ask yourself if a meeting is the right way to get the job done. Would a focused work session be a better alternative? A brainstorming group? A conversation with one or two colleagues? If you've ruled out all the other ways to accomplish your goal, then schedule your meeting. But once you've called the meeting, you become the Driver.

2. State the purpose of the meeting and back it up with a written agenda. All meetings should have a clear objective that is easily measured by the meeting's end, meaning you either achieved the goal (decision made, information gathered, etc.) or you didn't. If you didn't get what you wanted, schedule another meeting or find another way to get the desired result. But never go into a meeting winging it.

3. Invite attendees selectively. It's become a sort of corporate status symbol to get invited to lots of meetings. When you're the inviter, determine whether you really need a cast of thousands or if four or five people would accomplish more. At Amazon, Jeff Bezos has declared that no meeting should require more than two pizzas to feed all attendees. While that sounds like a breezy rule of thumb, there's solid evidence that the more people invited to a meeting, the more productivity goes down. On the flipside, if you are invited to more meetings than you can possibly attend, determine if you're really needed or if your presence is gratuitous. If it's the latter, politely beg off or send a subordinate.

4. Watch the timing. Just because a meeting is long, doesn't mean it's effective. Choose a timeframe that sends a "we mean business" message, like a twenty-two-minute meeting. Or consider a 10-15 minute "standing meeting" or "morning huddle" where everyone stays on their feet, literally, for the duration. Try an unusual start

time, like 9:19 am, to get people's attention. Then, start on time, resist the urge to backtrack to fill in latecomers, and end on time, resolution or not. People will not only be more willing to attend your meetings, but they'll come prepared.

5. Set strict guidelines and enforce them consistently. Once you've stated the meeting's purpose in a written agenda, invited the right people, and started the meeting on time, make sure you adhere to the objectives at hand, preferably three or less. If anything is off-topic, park it by writing it down on a "parking lot list" and assign ownership to someone to follow up at a later time. Ask your Organizer to create a decision log, information tracker, or project owner list, and write in relevant updates and next-step actions. Consider a no-electronics rule and ask people to leave cell phones and laptops behind. If the meeting is really twenty-two minutes or less, no one is going to miss anything earthshaking by ditching their gadgets. And when people see that your meetings lead to action and results, they'll be glad to participate. One of my clients, who heads a public relations firm, insists that her team not bring their mobile phones to staff meetings. If they can't park their cell phones for a brief time (which is often the case in the fast-paced world of media), she has them go back to work at their desks. No blame, no shame.

6. Put your positive foot forward. In her book *Broadcasting Happiness: The Science of Igniting*

and Sustaining Positive Change, author Michelle Gielan suggests that every meeting start with each participant bringing a positive observation to the table. She finds that this sets a tone for collegial interaction and collaboration—in essence, creating a hopeful community.

7. Have a little fun. Start your meetings with something unexpected once in a while: some food, a joke, an icebreaker, some swag, or a quick go-round about the weekend. Some fun tidbit that says while you mean business, you can still have a good time together. An occasional surprise lifts everyone's spirits and makes your meetings "not to be missed."[3]

THE CURSE OF COLLABORATION

Not all communication and collaboration happen at meetings, of course. According to research cited in the *Harvard Business Review*, time spent in collaborative activities in the workplace has grown by more than 50% over the past twenty years. While, on the surface, it seems positive that employees are working closely together, all that togetherness comes at a price. With daily tasks like email, phone calls, and meetings taking up as much as 80% of the typical employees' workday, very little time is left over for the actual work they must complete. Add to that how collabo-

---

3   Michelle Gielan, *Broadcasting Happiness: The Science of Igniting and Sustaining Positive Change* (Dallas: BenBella Books, Inc., 2015).

rative discussion time can slow down decision making and it's not hard to see why people get annoyed.

But all collaboration—and collaborators—is not equal. Check out these three distinct types. First, there's *knowledge collaboration*, where people are tapped for their skills and expertise. Second is *network collaboration*, where others are seeking connections and access to power. Third, *personal collaboration* is about offering one's time and energy to aid others.

So, what's wrong with collaboration? We should always be helpful when called upon, right?

Wrong. The balance is completely lopsided, with 20-35% of the collaborative efforts being shouldered by a mere 3-5% of employees. Not only is there an imbalance in the number of contributors, but the types of collaboration require different amounts of energy. While information and connections (as in the first two types of collaboration) can be passed along fairly easily, being approached for one's time and energy is far more challenging. And although the reputation and status of the person who is willing to go the extra mile for his or her colleagues are enhanced, it often comes at a price: namely, an onslaught of requests for time, access, and attendance at meetings that can wear out even the hardiest employee.[4]

In his book *Give and Take: Why Helping Others Drives Our Success,* author Adam Grant describes what he calls reciprocity styles of social interaction: giving, taking, and matching. He explains that most people shift easily

---

4   Rob Cross, Reb Rebele, and Adam Grant, "Collaborative Overload," *Harvard Business Review*, February 2016, https://hbr.org/2016/01/collaborative-overload.

between these roles. For example, you might be a giver when you're mentoring a young staff member, a taker when you're angling for a raise or promotion, and a matcher when you're sharing information with a peer. Interestingly, Grant tells us that givers are both the most and least successful of the three categories, with givers who can shift into taking and matching modes when appropriate the most successful of all.

You need to determine if your givers—that is, the collaborators in your group—are over-giving. Use employee engagement surveys or 360 assessments or plain old observation to see if you can determine what's working and what's not. Sometimes, the problem can be mitigated by simply shifting workload commitments more equitably. For example, if you know that Team Member Andi is drained by mentoring others, but Team Member Brian is energized by it, help them trade off activities so that they not only help others but also feed their engagement and enthusiasm.[5] You'll receive the additional benefit of helping your team develop their own leadership skills.

GETTING FEEDBACK THE OLD-FASHIONED WAY: ASKING FOR IT

It's not always easy to get the feedback you need to manage team projects or balance workloads, especially if you don't have access to engagement surveys or coaching programs.

5   Adam Grant, *Give and Take: Why Helping Others Drives Our Success* (Penguin Books, 2014).

Jessica Mah, CEO of San Francisco-based accounting software company inDinero, decided to get feedback by casually asking her employees how things were going and how she could help.

That was easy, Mah said, when she had only a dozen or so employees. But as inDinero grew to a team of two hundred people in five offices around the world, she found it much harder to get the feedback she wanted. So, she created the CEO Monthly Survey to ask everyone in the company:

- How's your manager doing?
- How happy are you?
- What questions/comments do you have for me?

She got surprisingly candid feedback from across the entire company that she could share with her managers, regularly letting them know what their "favorability ratings" and "team happiness scores" were. Of course, if you haven't set the tone for trust, no one is going to share the truth with you—it's just too great a risk. But when leaders like Mah care enough to *receive* feedback as well as give it, it makes for some pretty happy and hopeful team members.[6]

---

6   Jardley Jean-Louis, *How to Keep Getting Great Employee Feedback as Your Company Grows*, Video, The Playbook, 2017, https://www.inc.com/video/jessica-mah/how-to-keep-getting-great-employee-feedback-as-your-company-grows.html.

HOPEFUL HABITS

KEY TAKEAWAY #4

Teams are an essential construct of the workplace, but they can drain hopefulness, eventually affecting the entire organization. It is up to the team leader to keep the interaction positive and productive. Research shows that *how* teams communicate can often be as important as *what* they communicate.

HOPEFUL BELIEF #4

Take a look at the personalities described in *The Personality of High-Performance Teams* section above. What's your personality type? Can you identify the types of other people on your team? Is there a good mix, or are there too many of one type and not enough of another? How might you change the group to enhance productivity?

HOPEFUL BEHAVIOR #4

Even if you don't have MIT's electronic badge system to monitor team communication, you can determine how well it's working. Designate someone to be an observer and, if you want to keep this exercise under wraps until you've completed it, identify them as your notetaker. Have them sit in on a typical group meeting and record their observations on the *Five Factors of Effective Team Communication*. Are all team members talking and listening in equal measure? Do they face one another when they speak? Are they connecting with each other, including side conversations, and not just with the leader? Do they explore outside the group and share their insights?

Let your team know what you've learned about team communication and how *energy, engagement,* and *exploration* lead to success. Next, share your observations about your team and how you can improve your interactions. And, don't forget the fun!

Next, let's look at your personal leadership style to see how you can feed hope within your organization.

CHAPTER 5

YOUR LEADERSHIP SUPERPOWER

Bringing Out Excellence in Yourself and Others

"Once you choose hope, anything is possible."
—*Christopher Reeve*

When I first got my VP stripes and became department head for public relations and communications at Sony Pictures Television, I suddenly found myself overseeing a wide range of responsibilities, including corporate communications, television publicity, creative services, and special events. My team was as varied as my duties, from entry-level interns to senior publicists and copywriters. We juggled celebrity egos and executive demands, all while handling promotional launches for network comedies and dramas, cable movies, syndicated talk shows, live press events, and premiere parties.

Fortunately, I was able to hire my first real executive assistant in the form of brainy, ballet-loving Beth Levitin. Beth was hardworking, smart, and efficient, and could get along with just about anyone. Not only did she keep me from reeling off the planet with my crazy schedule and nonstop media deadlines, but she was also the perfect liaison to our creative and occasionally high-strung team.

I relied on Beth's competence and calm demeanor and often wondered what I'd do without her. Until one day I was faced with that reality. I was sitting in my office when Beth came in and shut the door. When you're a supervisor, you know that usually means one of two things: If it's one of your more problem-prone employees, they're about to lay a big headache in your lap. If it's one of your hardworking, self-managing staff members, like Beth, you go into immediate panic mode, fearing they might have been offered a better job elsewhere.

In Beth's case, it was neither of those things, but something far worse. She took a seat across from me, her face white as a sheet, and told me she'd just been diagnosed with a rare and very aggressive form of cancer called angiosarcoma. I didn't know it at the time, but subsequently learned that angiosarcoma is a cancer of the inner lining of the blood vessel that can travel through the system, occurring anywhere in the body, but is found most commonly in the skin, breast, liver, spleen, and deep tissue. Angiosarcomas are aggressive and tend to recur and spread, frequently resulting in tumor-related death.

As I tried to wrap my head around this tragic news, all I could think about was the ridiculous entertainment industry joke that got repeated whenever anyone took their role working on a game show or a sitcom a little too seriously, which was just about always: "It isn't the cure for cancer." That day, I sincerely wished I had that cure.

Despite the illness and the demanding treatment protocol that was prescribed for Beth, she was determined to continue working as much as she possibly could. She wasn't in denial—quite the contrary. Beth said that coming to work gave her a sense of purpose and hope. Now that you've learned about the future-focused nature of hope and the power of belief and expectation, you can probably understand why working was so important to Beth. I didn't get it at first, but as she explained why it meant so much to carry on with normal life as long as she could, it began to make sense.

For the next nine months, Beth received around-the-clock chemotherapy for one week out of every month. But despite the intensity of her treatment, this courageous young woman came into work every single day that she had enough strength to get out of bed. She'd often work until six o'clock, then go home and right to bed so she'd have enough energy to come back the next day and do it all over again. Even on the days when she'd start her week of chemotherapy, she'd still come to work straight from the hospital. She said that it wasn't until the next day or two, when the drugs kicked in, that she'd be too nauseated to get out of bed. She wanted to work while she was able.

I was in awe of what I came to view as Beth's unique *leadership superpower*—courage and grace under incredibly difficult circumstances—and so was my team. In what was probably the proudest period of my corporate life, we all joined in to pick up the slack at work, visit Beth in the hospital, and help her out at home. Most of all, my usually chatty group of PR folks honored Beth's desire for confidentiality and never shared a single bit of information about her illness with anyone outside our team. Not even when she came to work with a huge bruise on her cheek, visible through the cover-up she'd liberally applied, from fainting in the shower. Not even when her curly hair fell out and she replaced it with a silky, straight wig. And not even when her absences became so frequent I was forced to replace her with a long-term temp.

Instead, we closed ranks around her and made sure that both she and her job were cared for and protected until she got a clean bill of health and came back to work. Which, thankfully, she did. I'm happy to report that Beth is now healthy and happily married. My old team and I, Beth included, still hold regular "staff meetings," otherwise known as happy hour, at our favorite watering holes to talk about the old times and fill each other in on the new.

THE DUNNING-KRUGER EFFECT

All of us have a superpower—that is, a strength or talent that adds to our greatness. If we are insightful enough to recognize and capitalize on it, we can save an enormous amount of time and energy in terms of our professional development, like we saw with Jessica in chapter three. But many of us underestimate our own gifts and knowledge.

In fact, this psychological phenomenon is so common, it's been studied by numerous social scientists.

One of the more intriguing studies is named after two Cornell University scientists, David Dunning and Justin Kruger. The Dunning-Kruger effect tells us that the more expert you are in a particular field of study, the *less* likely you are to consider yourself an expert. Conversely, the newer you are to a field of study, the *more* likely you are to consider yourself an expert. Sounds crazy, right?

Dunning and Kruger explain it this way: With more than three billion people online, we have access to information and "instant expertise" more easily than ever before. When someone tackles a new skill or body of knowledge, they are often so enthusiastic about all they've learned, they tend to overestimate their mastery of the subject. They're so confident in their ability to learn their new subject, they become oblivious to the depth of information they actually have yet to conquer.

On the other hand, if someone is already expert in a subject, they are all too aware of the vast body of knowledge they still may have yet to learn and humbled by how limited their expertise actually is. Thus, novices tend to be surprised when they are wrong about something within their new field of interest, while experts are surprised when they are right about something in their chosen field.

Another element of this cognitive bias is the so-called experts' eagerness to "overclaim," stretching the truth with claims about their knowledge that don't hold up under scrutiny. Which explains why comics and late-night hosts, from Jay Leno to Jimmy Kimmel, have so much fodder for fun, asking unwitting guests questions about topics from sports to politics to parenting and taping their hilariously clueless responses.

What this means for you is be aware enough not to dismiss your legitimate expertise by undervaluing your skills and knowledge. Additionally, don't assume skills or understanding that you don't have, or you'll quickly be judged as inauthentic. Be prepared to say, "I don't know, but I'll get back to you once I get the information," or, "My team member Jill is actually the expert in that area, let's bring her into the conversation."

FEEDBACK FROM THE FOLLOWER PERSPECTIVE

Much of the leadership literature comes from studying what leaders can and should be doing, but it can be extremely helpful to see what leadership looks like from the other side of the desk. In their book *Strengths Based Leadership: Great Leaders, Teams, and Why People Follow*, authors and former Gallup executives Tom Rath and Barry Conchie tell us that what followers need from their leaders is often not what the company needs from them. Organizations need leaders who can articulate a vision, set strategies and priorities, build relationships, monitor progress, and course correct as needed. Yet when the study authors analyzed data from Gallup polls of more than ten thousand people, they discovered a completely different scenario.

The researchers conducted these studies using Gallup's standard Random Digit Dial (RDD) methodology, calling people at random and asking them two questions. Because this was a random poll and the only criterion was that the respondent had to be over eighteen, the data went beyond the workplace to include schools, community organizations, religious centers, and more.

First, participants were asked, "What leader has the most positive influence on your daily life?" Participants were then instructed to write down the initials of that person. Next, they were asked to "list three words that best describe what this person contributes to your life." By asking the participant to write down the initials of the leader, researchers guided them to isolate a specific person rather than answer in the abstract. As the respondent was asked to list specific contributions this leader made to their daily lives, it put the focus on the follower rather than the leader, as much of the past leadership research had done. It also lessened the probability that the respondent would cite a religious, sports, or political figure instead of someone they knew and interacted with personally.

Based on this research, the study authors determined four key themes that emerged most frequently as the attributes followers desire in their leaders. They are:

- Trust (which also included honesty, integrity, and respect)
- Compassion (which also included caring, friendship, happiness, and love)
- Stability (which also included security, strength, support, and peace)
- Hope (which also included direction, faith, and guidance)

Take a moment to think about these four key characteristics. It's pretty unlikely you've ever seen those words in a job description, yet that's what your followers really want from you. Now let's drill down a little deeper into each trait and see how well you're doing in each area.[1]

TRUST

Trust, or trustworthiness, is one of those things we know when we see but can't always quantify. Simply put, being trustworthy means others believe you have integrity, reliability, and an unconditional desire to do the right thing. It demands that the behaviors driven by those values are so unwaveringly consistent that others recognize and respond accordingly. In his book *The Speed of Trust*, Stephen M.R. Covey says, "Trust impacts us 24/7, 365 days a year. It undergirds and affects the quality of every relationship, every communication, every work project, every business venture, every effort in which we are engaged."[2] If you look back at the story in chapter four about Julia Rozovsky and the two teams she joined, it's obvious that there was a much higher level of trust in the case competition team, which allowed people to readily share ideas and voice opinions without judgement, than in the study group.

Ask yourself if:

---

1   Tom Rath and Barry Conchie, *Strengths Based Leadership: Great Leaders, Teams, and Why People Follow* (New York: Gallup Press, 2008).

2   Stephen M.R. Covey, *The Speed of Trust: The One Thing That Changes Everything* (New York: Free Press, 2006).

- Others regularly take you into their confidence and if you hold those confidences sacred.
- Your subordinates can easily come to you with problems, challenges, and even failures. Yes, it's great if they provide a remedy or recommendation along with the issue at hand, but it's critical that they trust you enough to tell you the truth.
- You elicit a sense of trust and respect among your teammates that allows for a free flow of information and creates an "I got your back" culture.

COMPASSION

Compassion is a deep sense of caring that goes beyond the professional relationship and demonstrates that you not only understand but also care about the personal well-being of your colleagues. Not only is it the right way to lead, in my opinion, but it's the smart way. There is plenty of research to support the conclusion that compassionate leaders increase engagement, boost productivity, and retain top employees. In research conducted at the Australian School of Business, which studied more than fifty-six hundred employees at seventy-seven organizations, the study authors found that the single greatest influence on productivity and profitability was leaders' ability to support, motivate, and develop team members so they rise to their highest levels.[3]

---

3   Christina Boedker, "The Rise of the Compassionate Leader: Should You Be Cruel to Be Kind?," *Business Think*, August 21, 2012, https://www.businessthink.unsw.edu.au/Pages/The-Rise-of-the-Compassionate-Leader--Should-You-Be-Cruel-to-Be-Kind.aspx.

Ask yourself if:

- Your concern for your team goes beyond the workplace. This is not to say you should butt in uninvited into their personal lives. But you should think of them as whole human beings inside and outside of work.
- You have a deep emotional understanding of what makes your team members tick. Where praise and recognition might motivate one person, another may be motivated by challenging stretch projects.
- You are rigorous about standards but kindhearted toward people. Leaders need to be able to have the tough conversations, to provide honest feedback and criticism, without making their colleagues feel belittled or humiliated.

STABILITY

If you've ever worked in an environment where you felt you were always on shifting sands, if not on the verge of an actual meltdown, you know what instability feels like. The stable leader provides a feeling of consistency and solidity that makes workers feel like they can settle in and build a career, or at very least, finish a project before the other shoe drops. Stable leaders are able to project a point of view while still being open to others' opinions. Their team knows they can count on them to make hard decisions, deal with higher-ups, and support them through ambiguity and change.

Ask yourself if:

- You can make the short-term decisions while keeping the long-term view in sight. Your colleagues want to know that you're going to stick around, even when the going gets tough.
- Your style and track record tell others that you're not out for yourself, but rather, that you want to help everyone succeed.
- You consistently recognize excellence with rituals and celebrations that create a fun culture that makes people want to come to work every day.

HOPE

This entire book is about how you can harness *true hope* to inspire others to join you in realizing a future-focused vision, even while acknowledging and overcoming the inevitable setbacks that occur along the way. Hope may be the thing with feathers, soaring and even magical, but it is not abstract or tenuous. Grounded in tough truths about *what is*, you might think of hope as not only having feathers, but talons. It lifts our sense of what is possible, but also gives us the tenacity to hold tightly to our vision despite the obstacles.

Ask yourself if:

- You help people create a behavior-based path to a better future at work and at home.
- You serve as a role model for others, motivating them with your commitment and caring.

- You inspire people to excel, rising to heights of which they never knew they were capable.

SUPERHERO LEADERSHIP

I love looking at heroes of myth, legend, and literature as role models for today's leaders. (You can read more about my literary doppelganger in my book *Traveling Hopefully*.) After all, if a hero from the time of Homer is still relevant today, there must be something of great value and meaning there. Let's have some fun that you can take back to your team by comparing your leadership superpower to some actual (okay, fictional) superheroes. Ask yourself which of these traits are part of your leadership style and how you can use them to make the workplace safe for mere mortals.

Superman

I'm no comic expert, but I'll wager that Superman is the best known and most beloved of all the superheroes. With his super strength, constant desire to do the right thing, and modest alter-ego persona, he sets the gold standard for other heroes. Yet, despite his Man of Steel strength, he shows his vulnerability in love and, most of all, to Kryptonite. *Like many power leaders, he balances strength with vulnerability.*

Wonder Woman

With superhero powers that go back to her birth among the Greek gods, the Justice League's Wonder Woman is a warrior princess of the Amazonian people. She has a breadth of training in strategy and combat, as well as an arsenal of tools, including the Lasso of Truth and her pair of indestructible wristlets. *A feminist icon dedicated to fighting injustice, she is a role model for women's leadership.*

Iron Man

More flawed than most superheroes, Iron Man is nonetheless one of the most creative thinkers of them all. A wealthy mogul, engineer, and playboy, Tony Stark relies on a powered suit of armor to keep him alive post-chest trauma. *An inveterate risk-taker, Iron Man's technological genius is his leadership strength.*

Wolverine

One of the X-Men, Wolverine is a mutant hero who can function as a solo operator or part of a team. His ability to heal his wounds, come back from defeat, and maintain his longevity make him a formidable foe. *Wolverine's regenerative abilities make him a resilient leader, able to take the blows and bounce back again and again.*

Invisible Woman

A member of the Fantastic Four, Invisible Woman uses light waves to make herself and others invisible. She can project fields of psionic energy as either an offensive or defensive force, making her very powerful without having super strength. *A wife, mother, sister, and working scientist, Invisible Woman, a.k.a. Sue Storm, is a great example of work-life balance in action.*

The Flash

Actually a few different superhero versions rolled into one, The Flash is known for his extreme speed in running, moving, and thinking. He uses his super-human speed, borne from a radioactive lightning ball that killed his mother, to combat criminals. By day, The Flash is a criminal investigator driven to avenge his mother's death and clear his father's name. *His leadership power is velocity, critical to success in today's swiftly changing world.*

Spider-Man

Defeat after defeat, Spider-Man keeps coming back for more. Although his wall-climbing abilities are truly remarkable, Spidey remains as humble as down-to-earth counterpart Peter Parker. A humorous and friendly self-made guy, he has no mentor and is completely self-taught in terms of his superpowers. *Spider-Man possesses one of the most important leadership skills of all: likeability.*[4][5]

THE ULTIMATE SUPERPOWER: LIKEABILITY

A colleague of mine, who happened to be one of the most

4   Josh Wilding, "10 Greatest Marvel And DC Comics Superheroes Of All-Time," *ComicBookMovie.com*, March 13, 2016, https://www.comicbookmovie.com/comics/marvel_comics/10-greatest-marvel-and-dc-comics-superheroes-of-all-time-a132032.

5   Ranker Community, "The Best Comic Book Superheroes of All Time," *Ranker*, accessed July 1, 2017, http://www.ranker.com/crowdranked-list/best-superheroes-all-time.

senior women in the television industry at the time, told me early in my career that I was "too nice for the business." It was clear that she didn't intend that as a compliment, and I was completely stymied by how being nice could be a deficit rather than an asset. While *nice* is often synonymous with *pushover*, which is probably closer to what she actually meant, I always considered likeability (my own included) to be an asset. Turns out the data bears out that assumption.

In the book *Likeonomics: The Unexpected Truth Behind Earning Trust, Influencing Behavior, and Inspiring Action*, author Rohit Bhargava makes an important distinction between *nice* and *likeable*. *Likeable* people, states Bhargava, are genuinely empathetic and honest, while *nice* people may tend to avoid unpleasant truths in an attempt not to offend others, which can make them less trustworthy and, ultimately, less likeable. Interestingly, on his website, Bhargava calls himself a brand strategist, trend curator, and "nice guy." Better make that "likeable" guy, Rohit.[6]

Not all great leaders are likeable, of course. Henry Ford, Steve Jobs, and former Uber CEO Travis Kalanik never won any popularity contests for their driven, dictatorial styles. Being likeable, such as Starbucks founder Howard Schultz or the inimitable Oprah Winfrey, doesn't mean you have to be warm and fuzzy, sugarcoating your directives or softening your blunt style. But it does mean that you should balance the demands of business with a level of kindness and transparency that allows people to maintain their dignity even in difficult circumstances.

---

6   Rohit Bhargava, *Likeonomics: The Unexpected Truth Behind Earning Trust, Influencing Behavior, and Inspiring Action* (Hoboken, NJ: John Wiley & Sons, Inc., 2012).

In a study conducted by management consulting firm Zenger Folkman, the study authors found that leaders who scored high on likeability were also rated as the most effective leaders by their colleagues. The researchers cited a significant parallel between a leader's likeability and their willingness to ask for, and then act on, feedback from others. The higher ratings were linked to more positive employment satisfaction and engagement scores, sales, customer service, and even job safety.[7]

ARE YOU A LIKEABLE LEADER?

So what makes a likeable leader? Depends who you ask, of course, but most human resource and leadership experts agree that it starts with self-awareness. Among the traits that likeable leaders have in common are humility and approachability; generosity of spirit; stability and sound judgment; the ability to connect emotionally; passion and a sense of purposefulness; and character.

Ask yourself the following questions to see how you score as a Likeable Leader. Note your responses and the corresponding points using the following key:

- Yep, I've got this. *Score 3 points*
- Kinda sorta. *Score 2 points*
- I could do a LOT better. *Score 1 point*

---

7   Zenger Folkman, "Zenger Folkman Likability Index" (Zenger Folkman, 2013), http://www.zengerfolkman.com/media/articles/ZFCo-WP-Likability-Index-040413.pdf.

1. If you make a promise to someone in your group, do you keep it?
2. Do you promote easy collaboration and open communication?
3. Are you trusted and respected by your team?
4. Do you give feedback that is both candid and constructive, without belittling the receiver?
5. Do you share the credit with others when things go well?
6. Do you take the blame when things go wrong?
7. Do you consciously set a good example through your words and actions?
8. Are you aware when your team members feel stressed or overloaded?
9. Do you know your employees as people, not just as professionals?
10. Do you attempt to keep a level playing field among your team members and avoid playing favorites unfairly?
11. Do you show vulnerability when appropriate?
12. Do you have a sense of humor, encouraging fun and laughter among your team?

Check below to get your Leadership Likeability score:

- 1-12 Barely Likeable Boss: Chances are you put your own needs before others, failing to give your teammates the encouragement and support they need to grow. Warm up your communication and make sure you treat people with respect and kindness.

- 13-24 Fair to Middling Manager: You're doing a decent job of demonstrating care and kindness to others, but it still leaves a lot to be desired. Fine-tune your leadership likeability with deep listening, positive role modeling, and direct feedback.

- 24-36 Inspirational Leader: Bravo! You're showing genuine care and concern for team members, an authentic desire to connect, and the ability to inspire others to grow and develop. Continue to help others as you build a culture of collaboration, trust, and respect.

HOPEFUL HABITS

KEY TAKEAWAY #5

Whether you're a new or seasoned leader, you need to know what your organization wants from you in terms of meeting business objectives, but you also need to understand what your followers want: trust, compassion, stability, and hope.

HOPEFUL BELIEF #5

Look back through this chapter to determine your *Leadership Superpower*. Are you a technology-driven leader? A leader who connects deeply with others? Maybe you're a great communicator or analyst. Write down what makes you truly great at what you do—and don't hold back. This is your time to shine a spotlight on your superhero strength.

HOPEFUL BEHAVIOR #5

Next, identify three actions that would make even greater use of your superpower. Determine a specific outcome (or outcomes) you want to achieve, and laser-focus your strengths and skills right at the core. Maybe you'll organize a training session to give everyone the latest tech updates to improve their productivity. Perhaps you'll use your communication super skills to kick off a new company newsletter or intranet. Whatever you decide to do, shift your superpower to high gear and get moving.

In chapter six, we'll take a deeper dive into communication skills, critical for leadership development, team building, and creating a hopeful culture.

CHAPTER 6

COMMUNICATING HOPE

The Power of
High-Impact Conversations

*"Wise men speak because they have something to say,
fools because they have to say something."*
—Plato

When I had the privilege of delivering a keynote address at the New Mexico Women's Symposium sponsored by nuclear enrichment company Urenco USA, I jumped at the chance to take a tour of their facility. After all, how often do you get to peek inside a plant that uses world-class centrifuge technology to provide uranium enrichment services so that its customers can generate low-carbon nuclear energy?

Urenco's Health and Safety Manager Jenise Dahlin

set me up with a radioactivity monitor that measured my levels before and after the tour (I was glad to note, there was no change). The first two things I noticed about the state-of-the-art facility were how few people actually worked inside the plant due to its sophisticated automation and, secondly, that it was so spotless I could have eaten off the floor. But what stayed with me long after my visit was the precision of communication I witnessed among facility personnel during even the most routine tasks.

Walking through the massive plant, which looked a bit like the bridge of a huge ship, I followed along, watching as two technicians worked together. One of them initiated a process with a verbal announcement of the procedure about to take place, the other technician responded back with a confirmation of the announcement, and then the first verbally confirmed the confirmation. In other words, it was an A-B-A check-and-balance where A: I say something, B: you confirm what I just said, and A: I confirm your confirmation.

In chapter four, we saw how critical communication skills are to teamwork, with the potential to foster trust, engagement, and collaboration. The ability to communicate accurately and persuasively is the foundation of building and maintaining positive relationships with others. It's the back-and-forth of daily discourse, whether it takes place in person, via phone, in writing, or by video, that deepens bonds, gets decisions made, and ensures productivity. And while good communicators aren't always good leaders, good leaders are nearly always good communicators.

Just think what would happen if we were as precise as the Urenco team in our everyday interactions, which, of course, most of us aren't. In this chapter, we'll explore effective communication—not just *what* you say but *how* you say it. When you begin to think about communication (whether it takes the form of a simple remark or something as sensitive as handling uranium) as a clear and concise exchange that leaves little room for misunderstanding, you have the essence of effective communication: *that the message you deliver is the same as the message that is received.* That kind of precision—where people are confident in the clarity of the exchange—contributes to a culture of hopefulness by creating a shared experience where teammates bond over actions and behaviors as they build toward the future together.

So, let's take a look at both the substance and style of effective communication, as well as some bad habits and blunders, starting with *your* communication style.

DISCOVERING YOUR PERSONAL COMMUNICATION STYLE

Just like there's no one way to be an effective leader, there are lots of communication styles that motivate others. My intention with this section is not that you choose a style that appeals to you, but that you enhance the style that you already have naturally. Take the following quiz and then score yourself using the key at the end to get some insights on your personal communication style.

1. You are asked to serve on a panel to address em-

ployee engagement within your organization. You decide to:

    a. Establish a task force to study engagement across business units.

    b. Create a science-based survey that will accurately measure engagement.

    c. Share concepts from world-class companies to learn from their best practices.

    d. Discuss how it feels to be a truly engaged employee.

2. You plan to hold a celebration to acknowledge your team for a great year-end. As part of your event, you:

    a. Create a PowerPoint deck that shows how far you've come in the last decade and why.

    b. Invite everyone to a fun company picnic where they can bring their families.

    c. Run progress reports on the various teams and recognize the top performers.

    d. Identify three major initiatives that will drive future progress even further.

3. A subordinate comes to you with a complaint about how women are undermined in the organization. You:

    a. Immediately alert HR and begin an investigation into the complaint.

    b. Begin planning for a major women's training initiative that will eventually roll out to all the female employees in the company.

    c. Sit the employee down and find out what happened and how you can help.

    d. Put together a task force to study the data on gender intelligence.

4. You believe the best way to run a meeting is to:
    a. Get people excited about future possibilities.
    b. Have a clear and focused agenda and stick to it.
    c. Let everyone offer a personal tidbit to increase camaraderie before you dive into the topic.
    d. Bring the latest data on the subject at hand and parse through it.

5. You get along best with people who:
    a. Think and talk in a linear fashion, connecting the dots between thoughts.
    b. Are creative thinkers who are able to easily talk about emotions.
    c. Back up what they say with facts and statistics.
    d. Think big and aren't afraid to take risks to get where they want to go.

6. You've had a disagreement with a peer that has caused a rift between your two departments. You:
    a. Offer to sit down with your colleague and talk it out as candidly as possible.
    b. Explain to your colleague precisely where you think he went off track.
    c. Catalogue the interactions with your colleague from the past six months and prepare an in-depth report about the facts in dispute.
    d. Tell yourself it isn't that big a deal in the long run and get back to work.

7. When there is a big decision to be made, you place your trust:
   a. In the numbers: they never lie.
   b. In your gut: it always steers you right.
   c. In the big picture: if we know where we're going, we'll figure out the rest.
   d. In slow and careful planning, looking at the downside as well as the upside.

8. When you're interviewing job candidates, you like to ask about:
   a. The person's upbringing—it can tell you a lot about who they are today.
   b. The jobs listed on their resume—you like to understand their entire career trajectory.
   c. Their career dreams and fantasies—they can tell you a lot about a person's motivation.
   d. What data they have to back up the claims they've made about their past career success.

9. At professional conferences, you're most likely to:
   a. Attend sessions that have a fact-based, data-rich approach to the topic.
   b. Reconnect with old friends and colleagues, making time to catch up on each other's lives.
   c. Connect with a few people who can have a significant impact on your career or the company.
   d. Study the agenda and find a cross section of sessions that will enhance your skills.

10. When you attend meetings, you typically:
    a. Help keep the meeting on track—you don't have much patience for digressions.

    b. Bring your laptop so you'll have all the data at your fingertips.

    c. Arrive 3-5 minutes early so you can chat with everyone before you get down to business.

    d. Keep things at a high strategic level—if you're not planning for the future, you don't need to be there.

11. Of these four leadership behaviors, your preferred style is to:

    a. Simplify complex research and analysis so everyone can apply it to their own areas.

    b. Get people excited about what you can accomplish if you all pull together.

    c. Hold people accountable for hitting specific milestones toward major goals.

    d. Recognize colleagues for their accomplishments, strengths, and skills.

12. Friends and coworkers often describe you as:

    a. Organized and detailed—you like to keep the trains on the track.

    b. Bold and inspirational—you help people see the big picture.

    c. Empathetic and kind—you bring out the best in others.

    d. Meticulous and data driven—you like precision.

Scoring Key

Now tally up your answers, using the key below, by noting the letter response for each question. For example, my responses fell into two categories: I scored 7 in Visionary and 5 in Connector. You'll learn more about what those categories mean in just a minute.

1. A/Functionary; B/Analyst;
   C/Visionary; D/Connector
2. A/Analyst; B/Connector;
   C/Functionary; D/Visionary
3. A/Functionary; B/Visionary;
   C/Connector; D/Analyst
4. A/Visionary; B/Functionary;
   C/Connector; D/Analyst
5. A/Functionary; B/Connector;
   C/Analyst; D/Visionary
6. A/Connector; B/Analyst;
   C/Functionary; D/Visionary
7. A/Analyst; B/Connector;
   C/Visionary; D/Functionary
8. A/Connector; B/Functionary;
   C/Visionary; D/Analyst
9. A/Analyst; B/Connector;
   C/Visionary; D/Functionary
10. A/Functionary; B/Analyst;
    C/Connector; D/Visionary
11. A/Analyst; B/Visionary;
    C/Functionary; D/Connector
12. A/Functionary; B/Visionary;
    C/Connector; D/Analyst

While you may have answers in all four categories (I had answers that fell into two of the four categories), take special note of your primary and secondary communication styles as you read the descriptions below.

- *The Connector*. If most of your answers fell into the Connector category, you're a relationship builder, highly self-aware as well as highly intuitive about other people's thoughts and feelings. Your colleagues typically find you a comforting and calming presence. You tend to be a very good listener, and people often come to you with their challenges. Whether or not you can solve the problem, you generally make the person feel better just by showing that someone else genuinely cares about what they're going through. Be aware that Analysts and Functionaries may find you a little too "touchy feely" for their taste, viewing you as relying too heavily on emotions rather than facts.

- *The Analyst*. If Analyst was your primary category, you are good with research, numbers, and technology. Many of you are excellent at synthesizing complicated data and explaining its relevance to others, who may not be as analytical as you are. Although many Analysts are found in finance, legal, research, and IT, they can excel in any area. Analysts aren't generally comfortable discussing emotions and, consequently, may appear a little chilly or unfeeling to others.

- *The Visionary*. If your answers fell mostly into the Visionary category (as mine did), you like to focus on the future and think about what's next for you, your team, and your organization. Your ability to predict trends is so strong, people sometimes think you can see around corners. Because you believe anything is possible if you put your mind to it, you are good at getting other people excited to join you. But be careful—sometimes your lack of attention to detail can get you into trouble and make others skeptical of your big-picture notions.

- *The Functionary.* Functionaries are the ones who make things happen. You are direct, process oriented, and have no qualms about holding people to task. Your take-no-prisoners attitude is appreciated by those who find comfort in rules and order, but you occasionally cause more emotional and creative types to chafe under your restrictive style. The need for systems is so obvious to you, you don't always take the time to explain why they're needed to others, so be sure to clue in your nonlinear thinkers and you'll all be on the same page.

Think about your primary style. Does it accurately reflect how you typically communicate? Or are you a blend of several different styles? How do you deal with colleagues whose styles are diametrically opposed to your own? How does your style affect your interactions with your colleagues and team members? Is it positive? Does it feed hope? Foster trust? Add to engagement and motivation?

TEN TENETS OF EFFECTIVE COMMUNICATION

When you understand that most business communication isn't about you, but rather about helping others meet their needs so they can add value to the organization, you will significantly reduce the number of communication problems you have. That said, communication is often slippery, vague, and idiosyncratic. And that's on a good day. Bottom line is that words mean different things to different people. Though communication, of course, encompasses a lot more than words. It includes context, tone, nonverbal behaviors, listening, and much more. Let's jump in and take a look at the principles that constitute effective communication.

Integrity and Trust

Though it may seem obvious, it's worth stating that successful communication starts with integrity. This includes accuracy with facts, data, and details, but also emotional honesty in terms of context and color. You can't demand trust—you earn it with integrity, but it's well worth the effort. When people feel that you are worthy of their trust, they'll open up and share information—including the negative stuff—much more freely. People who trust you will be far more understanding when you make an unpopular decision or a blatant misstep. But when you're not trusted, people will rarely forgive or forget when you make a mistake.

Crystal-Clear Specificity

If you've ever watched a leader drone on until you have no idea what they're talking about, and even less interest, you know how important it is to be clear and succinct. Think through—or even role-play—important conversations in advance, choosing your words wisely and weeding out the extraneous, whether verbally or in print. The more concrete and specific you can be with information, direction, and feedback, the more likely you are to have happy followers. Forget the corporate speak, industry lingo, and clever allusions. The world is complicated enough without your fancy communication making it even more so.

Hopefulness and Empathy

Even if you are a fact-loving Analyst or Functionary by nature, it's essential to connect emotionally with others. If you enter each interaction with an attitude of servant leadership, where the focus is legitimately on the other person's success, you'll help create a culture of hopefulness and caring. Set the tone for communications ranging from casual conversations to formal presentations by injecting warmth, empathy, and humor. When you focus on serving and contributing rather than directing and demanding, you'll make much deeper and more positive connections with colleagues.

Authenticity

There's a lot of truth in the beautiful Maya Angelou quote, "People will forget what you said, people will forget what you did, but people will never forget how you made them feel." As we're increasingly inundated with phony marketing messages and soulless robocalls, when we hear someone who we know instinctively is speaking from the heart, we're more likely to respond positively. Even though conventional wisdom tells us to keep our personalities, including the quirks and passions that make us who we are, in check at work, I believe just the opposite. Bring your true self—and that includes your vulnerable self—to work, and others will do the same.

Inclusivity

Diversity and inclusion are getting a lot of attention in the workplace these days. While some more progressive companies take their efforts in this regard very seriously, others give it mere lip service. Whatever your organization's stance, don't think of inclusivity as merely corporate responsibility. Rather, think of it as your personal mission to be as inclusive and accepting of other people as possible, including their opinions, temperaments, and experience. And that means the Naysayers, those wonderful contrarians who always seem to want to go against the grain. When you keep an open mind and listen to what they have to say, no matter how they say it, you may just strike gold.

Listening

While technology has made long-distance communication easier than ever, listening has sadly taken a backseat. Let's put it back up front where it belongs. Whether you're in a social or business situation, shut out all distractions and concentrate on the person speaking by focusing on their face as they talk. If you feel your attention getting diverted, zero in on their eyes. Connect with the speaker by genuinely caring about what he or she has to say. Listen to the intent behind the words and observe their body language and demeanor to get the full meaning. Be sure to fuel your focused listening with compassion and curiosity about the other person's point of view, including asking meaningful questions, and they'll return the favor when you're the one doing the talking.

Nonverbal Behaviors

You hardly need a scientific study to tell you the meaning behind a new acquaintance extending a friendly hand or a driver raising a middle finger when you cut them off in traffic. Our bodies are communicating continuously. Although we instinctively recognize many of the gestures and behaviors, it can be extremely useful in both business and social settings to increase your knowledge of nonverbal communication. For example, according to the authors of *How to Read a Person Like a Book,* out of two thousand videotaped negotiations, not one case reached a settlement when one of the negotiators had their legs crossed, a signal of being closed off to the other person. Harvard sociologist Amy Cuddy, in her TED Talk on *power poses*, tells us that people who spread out comfortably at the conference table are generally confident and at ease. Those who shrink into a ball, taking up as little space as possible, are ill at ease or fearful. Pay as much attention to what's not being said as to what is, and you're likely to pick up on levels of interest or lack of appeal, authenticity or lying behavior, confidence or insecurity, and much more.[1][2]

1 Gerard I. Nierenberg and Henry H. Calero, *How to Read a Person Like a Book* (New York: Pocket Books, 1971).
2 *Your Body Language May Shape Who You Are,* TED Video, TED, 2012, https://www.ted.com/talks/amy_cuddy_your_body_language_shapes_who_you_are.

Feedback

Getting and giving feedback is such an important topic, it comes up frequently among my coaching clients. While some organizations like Deloitte, Adobe, and Accenture have dumped traditional annual appraisals, thinking that too much emphasis was put on the past instead of the future, relevant and timely feedback will always be essential to developing talent. Personally, I believe in both ad hoc and formal feedback—whatever works within your culture and climate.

What most people don't realize, however, is that the *giving* is often as difficult, if not more so, than the *receiving*. For those on the receiving end, the rules are pretty straightforward: take all criticism gratefully but don't hesitate to ask questions if you don't understand or if you disagree with the feedback that is being offered. For the process to be truly useful, you need to be able to turn comments into action. Ask for examples and anecdotes that illustrate the behavior to be modified.

For those on the giving side of the feedback table, you may want to rethink the conventional wisdom of what's commonly called "the praise sandwich," where the negative commentary gets wedged between two slices of positive commentary. You may think you're taking some of the sting out of your complaint by adding some encouraging comments. But it's more likely that you're actually watering down your criticism to the point that the recipient can hardly recognize it for what it is: an opportunity to improve. Resist the urge to sugarcoat. Your job in giving feedback is not to make people *feel* better (though you'll find plenty of opportunities for that), your job is to help them *perform* better.

As we saw above, clarity is paramount. State your criticism clearly, give a specific example, and explain how you'd like it rectified or dealt with in the future. But don't succumb to feeling like you're the big, bad boss for telling it like it is. Be candid, but kind. It's okay to be tough on the subpar performance, but it's important to be kind to the person. Your goal is not to humiliate your employee, but to change the unwanted behavior. A study in *The Journal of Consumer Research* showed that the more expert the recipient, the more direct you can be in your feedback. Not that you need to use kid gloves with your more junior players, but be aware that they're still learning, and customize your feedback with that in mind.[3]

For example, if you're giving constructive criticism, you might say, "That wasn't the best way to handle the customer complaint. You kept them waiting for an answer for two days, and when you responded, your tone was far too brusque. In the future, please respond to all complaints within twenty-four hours. And when we're wrong, as we were in this case, we always give a sincere apology."

The feedback recipient might respond, "I see now that I didn't handle that well. In the future, I'll respond within one business day and I'll make sure my tone, including a sincere apology, is much friendlier." Of course, if your employee disagrees or has questions, you might hear, "I'm not sure I understand. The customer asked to speak to a

3   Stacey R. Finkelstein and Ayelet Fishbach, "Tell Me What I Did Wrong: Experts Seek and Respond to Negative Feedback," *Journal of Consumer Research* 39, no. 1 (June 2012): 22–38.

supervisor and I couldn't get anyone above me to respond right away. Is there something I might have done differently?" Remember that even if you disagree or question the feedback, your tone as the subordinate should still be professional and positive.[4]

Another element of giving constructive criticism is that your *feedback must be timely*. If there's an issue that needs to be discussed and/or corrected, your criticism should be offered either as soon as the infraction occurs or as soon as you learn of it. By hesitating, you send a message that it's not that big a deal or that you're too much of a wimp to criticize, neither a helpful perception. Of course, you want to give positive feedback and recognition, too. Instead of the praise model, where you lump the good and bad together, diluting both in the process, handle positive feedback the same way you would negative. When an employee does something great, let him know, specifically and immediately. And share the win with others. For example, "Terrific email this morning, Jim. I loved how you summed up the meeting for everyone. I'm going to let the boss know how helpful it was."

Feed your feedback culture by letting your team members know it's always okay to ask for feedback. Model the appropriate way to ask without seeming like an approval-seeking suck-up. That is, "Hey, let me know what you thought about how I conducted the off-site retreat. I'd love any notes you have so I can make the next one even more productive."

---

4   Stacey R. Finkelstein and Ayelet Fishbach, "Tell Me What I Did Wrong: Experts Seek and Respond to Negative Feedback," *Journal of Consumer Research* 39, no. 1 (June 2012): 22–38.

Presentations

There are multiple modes of communication, of course, beyond the one-on-one or small group discussion. Leaders and managers are often required to speak to large numbers of people, to conference via video because of time zone and geographical gaps, or to deliver formal presentations at client-facing or industry events. Again, the best communicators are able to connect, projecting energy, warmth, and feeling, whether they're speaking to ten people or ten thousand.

I know how daunting this can be, especially for leaders who haven't done much public speaking. As a professional speaker myself, I can tell you that it gets easier with time. Look for as many opportunities to present as possible, whether those are at a town hall, sales meeting, or internal training session, so you can get comfortable with being center stage.

Prepare your remarks carefully, then let go of the script and trust that you know your material. There's nothing that puts a roadblock between you and your audience faster than reading from a script. Use notes or a PowerPoint deck as a guideline, but don't keep your eyes glued to them. Have your internal communications rep work with you or hire an outside media or speaking trainer to help you with content and delivery. Videotape your presentation to see what's working and to improve upon what's not. For speaking newbies, try joining your local Toastmasters group. There are nearly sixteen thousand chapters in 142 countries with approximately half a million active members, and it's a safe, low-risk place to hone your speaking skills.[5] Trust me, the more you present, the easier it gets.

Writing Skills

According to Bryan Garner, author of the *HBR Guide to Better Business Writing*, the first goal of business writing is to make it clear *why* you're writing. Clarify your objective, address your audience appropriately, and state the outcome you're hoping for. For example, one of my entertainment clients needed to let a group of employees know that their offices would be moving. Since the team worked flex hours and were hard to call together face-to-face, she wrote a concise but friendly email to tell them, "Our CEO has determined that our division will run much more efficiently if we're in closer physical proximity to one another. To achieve that, we'll be moving everyone in our valley locations into our main city building. While we know the extra commute time may be an inconvenience for some of you, we're positive that the increased productivity will be worth it. Please call or come chat with me if you have any concerns you'd like to discuss." She informed them about the move (objective) and stated her hoped-for outcome (increased productivity). Simple, straightforward, and compassionate toward those who ended up on the losing side of the equation.[6]

By being professional and concise, and avoiding corporate speak, your readers will feel that they're being

5 Toastmasters International, "Toastmasters International," *Toastmasters International*, accessed July 1, 2017, http://www.toastmasters.org.

6 Bryan A. Garner, *HBR Guide to Better Business Writing*, HBR Guide Series (Boston: Harvard Business Review Press, 2012).

addressed by a living, breathing person and not an organization. Write your first draft quickly (sometimes it's hard to get started), then revise and revise again. If it's important, always let someone else review your work. Remember that spellchecker software won't pick up on the difference between "there" and "their" (my pet peeve) or "it's" and "its," so it's best to have a human with good editing skills take a peek at your work. Leave the humor and sarcasm to the comedians—they rarely work in print anyway. And no matter how succinct you think you're being, cut out any unnecessary words.

WHEN BAD COMMUNICATION HAPPENS TO GOOD PEOPLE

Despite all best efforts, revisions, and dress rehearsals, communication still goes awry at times. See if you've experienced a scene similar to this one play out at work or at home.

> *Supervisor: "I'd like to see a draft of the Roberts presentation this afternoon, if you can get to it before our 4 pm meeting."*
>
> *Supervisee: "Sure thing, Boss. I'll let you know how it goes."*

The 4 pm meeting rolls around and the boss says she wants to go over the pitch deck for the Roberts presentation. Completely taken by surprise, the employee working on the deck nearly has a meltdown, saying, "You told me to work on it *if* I had time. But I had to finish the talking points for the CEO's speech. I didn't know we'd be going over the pitch at this meeting." The boss, equally surprised, replies, "But I clearly said we were discussing it at 4 today."

You think you're on exactly the same page as someone else, only to discover they have an entirely different recall of the interaction you had moments before. Both sides are disappointed and left wondering how the other person could have gotten it so wrong. Too many of these miscommunications, and trust begins to slip.

Now, let's rewind the tape and try it again.

> *Supervisor: "I'd like to see a draft of the Roberts presentation this afternoon, if you can get to it before our 4 pm meeting."*
>
> *Supervisee: "I'm working on the talking points for the CEO right now. Should I put that aside and finish the Roberts draft for our 4 pm meeting?"*
>
> *Supervisor: "Yes, please. See you—and the draft—at 4!"*

Other common communication missteps include not making eye contact with the listener or, worse, multitasking on your phone or tablet during a conversation. Does anything show less respect than someone who can't stop texting during a business meeting or dinner with loved ones? Way to let the world know that everyone else is more important than the person right in front of you. Constantly interrupting, droning on endlessly, and playing one-upmanship ("I can top that!") are also annoying habits, but they can be cured with some mindful self-awareness. Audio- or videotape yourself, get some candid feedback from others, and see how you might change these behaviors.

Another bad habit many of us need to break concerns the use of filler words, all too common in today's sloppy speech patterns. These fillers include umm, ah, like, you know, and other stalls you use when your brain is catching up to your mouth. One physician friend who teaches a class on bedside manner to medical students told me he counts the number of filler words his residents use when they're presenting during rounds to make sure they understand that these verbal tics significantly reduce their credibility. His top score during a ten-minute grand rounds presentation was twenty-two filler words—ouch. Why not tape an impromptu speech or upcoming presentation and count how many um's and ah's you include?

Last but not least—do I really need to say it?—never escalate a problem via email or text. Those modes of communication lack tone, context, and frankly, basic good manners. If you're in close enough proximity, stroll down to the other person's cubicle and politely get whatever you have to say off your chest, leaving the listener an opportunity for rebuttal. If you're not nearby, pick up the phone or use a video-conference line, where tone of voice and positive nonverbal cues can help mend professional fences.

HOPEFUL HABITS

KEY TAKEAWAY #6

The essence of effective communication is that the message you deliver is the same as the message that is received. Simple, but not necessarily easy. Practice this skill, and it will enhance everything you do in both personal and professional life.

HOPEFUL BELIEF #6

Assess your own communication skills, noting one key strength and one area of improvement. Share your thoughts with at least three colleagues and see if they agree or disagree with your assessment. Ask them how they think you can improve as a communicator.

HOPEFUL BEHAVIOR #6

Assign yourself a communication stretch goal based on the feedback you received. Join your local Toastmasters group or offer to give a presentation at work. Also try practicing the A-B-A communication process by ending every conversation in which information is exchanged or an agreement is reached with a clear, agreed-upon summary statement.

In chapter seven, we'll look at some special considerations for women in the workplace. But, please note, this chapter is just as relevant for men—if not more so—than it is for working women.

CHAPTER 7

BEYOND BIAS

Hope and Tools for Women in the Workplace

"To handle yourself, use your head;
to handle others, use your heart."
—*Eleanor Roosevelt*

"I'm like the woman who pops out of the cake," sports-caster, author, and speaker Kate Delaney told me. "I'm used to popping up to take on a new challenge and hearing people say, 'I didn't know she could do that.' I've gotten used to being underestimated." She's rarely underestimated anymore now that she is the number one female sports commentator, talk show host, author, and speaker in the world of sports broadcasting. But it took more than five years and five hundred rejections to get on the map.

Kate's first big break came when she was working at a television station in the seaside town of San Luis Obispo, California. The sports anchor was going on vacation and suggested that Kate fill in on the sports desk while he was gone, even lobbying the news director on her behalf. The news director reluctantly agreed to give Kate a shot. Having received so much rejection, Kate was understandably nervous, but "clinging to hope," she jumped in. She prepped her sportscast and took her seat, one male crew member eye-rolling a girl behind the sports desk, while another was cheering her on with a big "Go Kate!"

Things were going smoothly at first, but when it came time for Kate to report on Mets pitcher Dwight "Doc" Gooden's recent back injury that was keeping him on the bench, instead of citing Gooden's "bulging disc," she mentioned his "bulging dick." It's one thing to flub your lines, but it's another thing altogether to flub them on air. Undeterred, Kate kept right on going, finished the broadcast, and then did a second one flawlessly. The news director, not to mention countless fans who called the station, thought she was terrific.

"Before that," stated Kate, "I could have wallpapered my apartment with rejection letters." She credits her willingness to ignore her own insecurities and keep her eye on the future for getting her where she is today. "Women were so fearful on my behalf," she said. "But I refused to let that negative vibration get in my head. Instead, I looked past the people who were unsupportive and stayed connected to the advocates, including plenty of men who helped me along the way."

It was a successful strategy, as Kate went on to host her own daily sports show, becoming the first woman ever to solo host a sports radio talk show in not one but two top ten markets—WFAN in New York City and KRLD in Dallas. She has interviewed more than twelve thousand people in her twenty-year career in radio and television, including four former presidents *and* LeBron James. Kate recently wrote a trivia book with sports stats and facts for women called *Invade the Man Cave*. As, indeed, she has.

THE TRUTH ABOUT UNCONSCIOUS BIAS

In this chapter, we'll look at some of the biases women face in the workplace and what you can do about them. Fair warning: if you feel like you've heard any of the following before, it's possible that you have. Women may have come a long way since we got the vote in 1920, but not nearly as far or as fast as many hoped. Yet it is hope—our future-focused vision—that keeps us forging ahead, bit by bit, to get where we want to go.

For starters, most men don't even acknowledge the gender issues that exist within their own organizations. According to research based on three thousand US businessmen and women conducted by Sylvia Ann Hewlett, economist and founder of the Center for Talent Innovation, 56% of men think that women have made "considerable progress" in the workplace over the past ten years. Only 39% of women, however, share that perspective. The truth is that women's career advancement has increased at gla-cial speed, with the number of women in senior executive positions hovering around 20% for the past decade. While most women recognize this disparity, the majority of men are blissfully unaware.[1][2]

Social scientists refer to this phenomenon—where men look around the workplace, see plenty of women, and assume the problem has been largely resolved—as gender fatigue or gender blindness. With all those women in the office, men assume that their organizations have done a decent job advancing the careers of their female counter-parts. Not so.

Sadly, what they don't see are the types of jobs in which women often find themselves stuck: administrative and support jobs, staff or "back-office" positions, and middle management. Many men are unaware that the vast number of professional women are not in jobs with profit-and-loss or strategic responsibilities that will put them in line for career growth, let alone for a shot at the C-suite. In fact, most men don't believe that gender bias even exists. While 49% of women—yes, nearly half—believe that bias is still an issue, only 28% of men agree with that assessment. Frankly, I'm shocked that only half of working women acknowledge the existence of gender bias. All men and women need to do is take a look at the pipeline, which

1   Jeffery Tobias Halter, "The Barriers to Advancing Women: What Men Aren't Seeing," *SmartBrief*, September 13, 2016, http:// www.smartbrief.com/original/2016/09/barriers-advancing-wom-en-what-men-arent-seeing?utm_source=brief.
2   Sylvia Ann Hewlett et al., "The Sponsor Effect: Breaking Through the Last Glass Ceiling" (Harvard Business Review, January 12, 2011).

we'll get to in a moment, to see how far women still have to go and how the odds continue to be stacked against them.

It's not just a matter of social and political fairness that suggests that women should play an equal role in leadership. It's also a matter of economics. It's been well documented that companies with women on their boards increase the bottom line. In fact, one study shows that simply by adding women to all-male corporate boards in India, the United States, and the United Kingdom, those countries could add $655 billion to their coffers. Even more significant, a recent study by McKinsey & Company, an international consulting firm, estimates that if women, who constitute half of the world's working-age population, were to earn wages equivalent to men, we would increase the global economy by a staggering $12 trillion or more.[3][4]

So with all this data, including a compelling case for increasing the world economy, why haven't we done a better job with gender parity?

The reasons are deeply rooted, multilayered, and culturally complex. Psychologists and social scientists who have researched bias have concluded that it has developed over the years as part of our brain's early warning system. When we are deluged with information about our circum-

---

3 Jonathan Woetzel et al., "How Advancing Women's Equality Can Add $12 Trillion to Global Growth," *McKinsey & Company*, September 2015, http://www.mckinsey.com/global-themes/ employment-and-growth/how-advancing-womens-equality-can-add-12-trillion-to-global-growth.

4 Francesca Lagerberg, "The Value of Diversity," *GrantThornton*, September 29, 2015, https://www.grantthornton.global/en/ insights/articles/diverse-boards-in-india-uk-and-us-outperform-male-only-peers-by-us$655bn/.

stances, including possible predators, escape routes, the environment, and so forth, we don't have time to process all the variables that would allow us to reach a rational conclusion. By then, we'd likely be dead. Instead, our brains make assumptions based on our history and experiences so we can shave a few life-saving seconds off the decision-making process.

This is what is known as *negativity bias*. Our brains respond far more strongly to negative input than to positive. So while we may hasten to run from a potential enemy, if we see a tasty bit of fruit hanging from a tree along the way, we're likely to pass it by in favor of getting out of the predator's path. Our survival instinct outweighs our hunger. Thus, assumptions, which blossom over time into deeply embedded biases, or patterns of preference and prejudice, become a powerful part of our survival instinct.

The unconscious biases formed by our upbringing, education, and cultural influences are so common in the workplace that they're woven into our DNA as a kind of corporate shorthand, where we come to believe that it's okay for men to be hired for *potential* while women are hired for *track record*. Or for men to be considered *strategic* while women are labeled *nurturing*. Sometimes these instances are overt, and other times they're more subtle or even unintentional, such as Google naming fourteen out of fifteen conference rooms on one floor after male scientists, ignoring the fact that there are many female scientists they might have chosen as inspirational namesakes.[5]

---

5   AON, "How Can We Beat Unconscious Gender Bias In The Workplace?" *The One Brief*, accessed July 1, 2017, http://www.theonebrief.com/how-can-we-beat-unconscious-gender-bias-in-the-workplace/.

While Google made a gender-sensitive gesture in renaming its conference rooms to include women, Silicon Valley companies have been under fire for years for what's known as the "bro culture." The bro culture is one in which young males are empowered, typically by their venture capital investors, to grow their businesses as quickly as possible by any means necessary, including skirting regulations and ignoring employee complaints.

A recent, but by no means isolated, example is that of ride-sharing company Uber. Brash and bratty former CEO Travis Kalanick became as famous for sexual harassment suits against the company as he did for Uber's disruptive transportation model. And who can forget the video-gone-viral of Kalanick berating an Uber driver, his own employee, for trying to discuss problems within the organization?

Stated author Dan Lyons in a 2017 *New York Times* opinion piece, "Bro cos become corporate frat houses, where employees are chosen like pledges, based on culture fit." He acknowledges that women do get hired, yet they rarely get promoted. Instead they become like the "sorority sisters" to the frat boys. Minorities (other than Asian males) and older workers are typically excluded altogether.[6]

So how do we right the ship? Awareness is a good start, but it isn't nearly enough to eradicate systemic bias within organizations. Nor are the typical one-day gender intelligence training sessions some companies employ. Institutions and individuals must undertake the hard work of rooting out biases—including their own—through

6 Dan Lyons, "Jerks and the Start-Ups They Ruin," *The New York Times*, April 1, 2017, https://www.nytimes.com/2017/04/01/opinion/sunday/jerks-and-the-start-ups-they-ruin.html.

ongoing checks and balances, the use of objective data, and the active pursuit of heterogeneous hiring patterns. The goal for hiring managers and corporate leaders must be to embrace diversity and inclusion in their representation of women, including women of color and the LGBT community, who are the most underrepresented of all. As Nichole Barnes Marshall, global head of diversity and inclusion at risk management firm Aon, said, "Diversity is counting heads; inclusion is making heads count."[7][8]

THE PROBLEM WITH THE PIPELINE

The short answer to the questions about why women don't reach the career heights that men do and why their trajectory is so much slower is that 1) men are hired and promoted more often than women and 2) at senior levels, women tend to shift from line to staff jobs that don't put them in line for the C-level positions. But the problem starts much sooner than that.[9]

Researchers from Sheryl Sandberg's nonprofit Lean In organization and McKinsey & Company conducted a survey of thirty-four thousand employees from 132 companies that was compiled into a report called *Women*

7   AON, "How Can We Beat Unconscious Gender Bias In The Workplace?" *The One Brief*, accessed July 1, 2017, http://www.theonebrief.com/how-can-we-beat-unconscious-gender-bias-in-the-workplace/.

8   S. Plous, "Understanding Prejudice," *Implicit Association Test*, accessed July 1, 2017, http://www.understandingprejudice.org/iat/index2.htm.

9   Lareina Yee et al., "Women in the Workplace 2016" (Lean In and McKinsey & Company, n.d.).

in the Workplace. While their findings, in keeping with other studies, showed a modest uptick in women's professional advancement over the past few years, they also demonstrated that most women fall behind their male counterparts early in the game and stay behind for the duration of their careers.

While men and women enter the workforce in nearly equal numbers, with men at 54% and women at 46%, the downhill slide for women begins shortly after. Next comes the widest gap, where 37% of women, compared with 63% of men, make the jump from entry level to manager, meaning that far fewer women are able to make that first, crucial step on the path toward senior leadership. From there, 32% of women reach senior manager/director, 29% make the critical VP rung of leadership, 24% get to the senior VP spot, with a mere 29% of women versus 81% of men hitting the C-suite.

THE MEDIA'S INFLUENCE ON GENDER BIAS

It's not just the corporate world where we see these levels of gender inequality. Once you become aware of the stereotypes, you begin to see them everywhere. Let's take a look at the entertainment industry, where I spent my first career, which is a microcosm of gender inequality in terms of not only what happens onscreen but also what happens behind the camera. Hollywood often gets a bad rap for perpetuating stereotypes, but there's an argument to be made that it's simply a reflection of our broader culture. Either way, its influence, particularly on children who take in seven or more hours of screen time per day, is unmistakable. With women either invisible or disproportionately depicted in G-rated films as small waisted, big breasted, and scantily clothed, it's not surprising that girls grow into women who are fixated on weight, body image, and career limitations.

It's not much better for films and television shows aimed at older audiences. Model-turned-actress-turned-women's-advocate Geena Davis is the founder of the Geena Davis Institute on Gender in the Media. She has been one of the single greatest forces for creating awareness about bias in the media and offering solutions for counteracting it. The tagline on her website SeeJane.org states, "If she can see it, she can be it," reminding studio executives of the power they hold to transform the dramatic imbalance in gender portrayals with regard to physical appearance and work/life aspirations. Among the Institute's findings, Davis and team point out that while women comprise 51% of the world's population, women are featured in only 31% of speaking roles in films, only 23% of film protagonists are women, and a mere 10% of films have a gender-balanced cast.

To date, Davis's Institute has generated the largest body of research on gender representation in family entertainment looking back over the past 25 years. Not only have they amassed and shared these resources, but they've had a significant impact on the media industry. Nearly 70% of industry executives knowledgeable about the Institute's research have altered two or more of their projects to be more gender accurate, while 41% have changed four or more of their projects. Changes to films such as *Inside Out*, *Equity*, and *The Little Prince* include altering the female character's career aspirations, professions, dialogue, and story arc, as well as an overall increase in the inclusion of women characters.

Some countries have gone a step further. Sweden has introduced a ratings scale, similar to those for sex and violence, based on what's referred to as the "Bechdel test." Named for cartoonist, graphic novelist, and playwright Alison Bechdel, to pass the test a film must have at least two named female characters who talk to each other about something other than a man. While some cinema fans feel the test goes a bit too far, proponents point out that the popular films that would flunk include the entire *Star Wars* franchise, the *Lord of the Rings* trilogy, the *Social Network,* and many more.[10]

Think about the movies and television series you've seen recently featuring female leads. Not as easy as coming up with male leads, I know, but give it a try. See if you recognize some of the more common negative stereotypes perpetuated by film and TV:

- **Evil Boss-Lady.** In this category, women who seem to have ice-cold blood running through their veins are in charge. Like Meryl Streep in *The Devil Wears Prada* or Jennifer Aniston in *Horrible Bosses,* these women leaders are portrayed as cunning, ruthless, and vindictive.
- **Hooker with a Heart of Gold.** There's no shortage of these stereotypes, going all the way back

10 Associated Press, "Swedish Cinemas Take Aim at Gender Bias with Bechdel Test Rating," *The Guardian*, November 6, 2013, https://www.theguardian.com/world/2013/nov/06/swedish-cinemas-bechdel-test-films-gender-bias.

to saloon owner Miss Kitty in the long-running TV show *Gunsmoke*. Since then we've seen a string of kind-hearted prostitutes, such as Julia Roberts, as Vivian, hoping to win over businessman Edward, played by Richard Gere in *Pretty Woman*, Anne Hathaway as hooker/loving-mother Fantine in *Les Miserables*, or Nicole Kidman as the dying hooker heroine Satine in *Moulin Rouge*.

- **Damsel in Distress.** The women-in-jeopardy genre, long a staple of made-for-television movies, includes women who are kidnapped, raped, or imprisoned—sometimes all three—by a notorious antihero. In need of rescue, assuming the assailant himself doesn't become the rescuer, they await the appearance of the prince, cop, or boyfriend who saves the day. Think Robin Wright in *The Princess Bride* or Belle in *Beauty and the Beast*.

- **Desperate Single Gal.** These anxious females will do just about anything—including diminishing their own identities—if it means they'll win the heart of the man of their dreams. Ariel in *The Little Mermaid* is willing to trade in her voice for a pair of legs so she can go get her guy; Meg Ryan gives up the job she loves as well as present-day Manhattan to go back in time with her prince charming in *Kate and Leopold*.

- **Women as Makeover Projects.** In this Pygmalion-esque style, women are willing to allow the men to transform them, often in the guys' own image, such as Audrey Hepburn as the aspirational Eliza Doolittle in *My Fair Lady* or Olivia Newton-John as Sandy, the good girl dying to be bad for Danny Zuko in *Grease*.

- **Hot Mamas.** Oversexualized and on the prowl, all four leads in *Sex and the City* gleefully objectify themselves as well as the men they're after. African-American and Latina women are often boxed into this category, such as Vivica Fox as the simmering jezebel in the film *Booty Call* or Sofia Vergara as the spicy sexpot in *Modern Family*.

This is not to say that we can't enjoy these film and television projects. But we should do so with an understanding of the subliminal and overt messages they're sending to us, and particularly, to our children. When DC Entertainment's *Wonder Woman* starring Gal Godot, who was both a combat trainer for the Israel Defense Force and Miss Israel, was released in June 2017, it became a huge box-office hit, prompting a *New York Times* editorial to query, "Asking Girls and Boys, What Would Wonder Woman Do?" Not only did the piece encourage parents to take their daughters to "witness the next-level girl power of the title character and the Amazons who raised her," but to not leave their sons at home. As the piece's author, Lisa Damour, pointed out, viewing *Wonder Woman* as a family could open lines of discussion not only about strength and compassion, but also about the differences and similarities of male and female superheroes. Seeing Diana stand up for herself as she stands up for the rights of others is a valuable lesson for anyone, young or old, male or female.[11]

The *Wonder Woman* movie, which took the number one spot in opening-weekend worldwide box office in the summer of 2017, brings up another issue faced by women in entertainment. As pointed out by Davis's research, as well as other studies, women are also woefully underrepresented behind the camera. Across 1,565 content creators (the people behind the making of film and TV projects), only 7% of directors, 14% of writers, and 20% of producers are women—meaning that there is only 1 woman working behind the scenes for every 4.8 men. Not a great ratio, despite the hits that women performers and directors have achieved in films like *The Hurt Locker*, *Big*, *Zero Dark Thirty*, *Shrek*, and more.

Just as Wonder Woman vanquished her movie foes, perhaps the *Wonder Woman* movie can vanquish some of the myths about women in the industry and women in the audience. Those myths include the idea that women won't go see a female superhero movie, particularly after previous films like *Elektra* and *Catwoman* flopped. Really? Then why did *Wonder Woman* rake in a weekend domestic gross box office of $100.5 million and $233 million worldwide, beating *Iron Man*, the first *Thor* and *Captain America* films, *Guardians of the Galaxy*, *Doctor Strange*, and a batch of *Spider-man* and *X-Men* sequels?[12]

---

11 Lisa Damour, "Asking Girls and Boys, What Would Wonder Woman Do?" *The New York Times*, June 8, 2017, https://mobile.nytimes.com/2017/06/08/well/family/asking-girls-and-boys-what-would-wonder-woman-do.html?smid=tw-share&_r=0&referer=https%3A%2F%2Ft.co%2FV4LsFNOZn6.

12 Box Office Mojo, "Superhero," *Box Office Mojo*, accessed July 1,

Not only did *Wonder Woman* reap the biggest opening ever for a female director with Patty Jenkins at the helm, but according to *The Hollywood Reporter*, while most superhero films count on at least 60% of their audience being composed of men, *Wonder Woman*'s audience was made up of 52% women and 48% men, thus busting another myth and proving that women will, indeed, come out for a well-directed superhero film with a female lead. Yet, unlike her male director counterparts, who typically sign multipicture deals when embarking on a potential blockbuster or even after they've had a flop or two, Jenkins was signed to a one-picture deal when she undertook *Wonder Woman*. Fortunately for her, the success of *Wonder Woman* all but ensures the continuation of the franchise in sequel-loving Hollywood, leaving Jenkins lots of leverage for any upcoming negotiations.[13][14]

WHAT ARE THE SOLUTIONS FOR INDIVIDUALS AND INSTITUTIONS?

Although lots of thoughtful companies are holding women's leadership events to increase skills and solidarity, those

2017, http://www.boxofficemojo.com/genres/chart/?id=superhero. htm&sort=opengross&order=DESC&p=.htm.

13 Pamela McClintock, "'Wonder Woman' Box Office: Where It Ranks in the Superhero Pantheon," *The Hollywood Reporter*, June 4, 2017, http://www.hollywoodreporter.com/heat-vision/wonder-woman-box-office-ranks-superhero-pantheon-1010063.

14 Nina Zipkin, "The Success of 'Wonder Woman' Speaks Volumes About Opportunity," *Entrepreneur*, June 6, 2017, https://www.entrepreneur.com/article/295384.

events alone won't change the landscape. First, organizations need to acknowledge that gender parity is a business issue, not just a women's or family issue. And it's not going to be remedied by throwing a few volunteers and a few thousand dollars into an initiative and then calling it a day. After all, what major company would launch a product or program with a tiny budget and a small group of volunteer supporters? Don't get me wrong, I'm a big fan of women's conferences, and have keynoted across the world for companies including Genentech, Honda, Intel, Kellogg's, Medtronic, Microsoft, and many more. But I don't kid myself that those forums are in themselves a solution. Rather, they are awareness builders and rallying cries for women—and men—to get involved.

But there are plenty of things we can do. Those in power within their organizations can make institutional changes to transform wage equality and hiring practices. Even individuals with little or no institutional leverage have far more power than they may realize. Here are some practical solutions for facing these complex issues head on.

- **When hiring, focus on specific skills and measurable criteria.** Eliminate as much subjectivity as possible in hiring and developing people. Anonymizing hiring decisions could be one way to help overcome gender-based hiring. In the world of music, blind auditions have been shown to increase the number of female musicians hired by orchestras by as much as 25-

30%. Think how huge that gain would be in a tech company or law firm.[15]

- **Rely on data to guide you.** Use the numbers to guide you. At Medtronic, for example, CEO Omar Ishrak made a declaration that he wants gender parity in terms of men and women in senior leadership roles by 2020. Although he originally stated that he wanted 50-50 parity by 2020, his appreciative but pragmatic team scaled that back to a 40-60 ratio. When you know your company's numbers—for good or for bad—you can use them to help you make your case.

- **Be aware of microaggression messages.** These subtle slights and put-downs are hurtful and unfair, yet tend to justify ill treatment of women. As with the "bro culture" discussed previously, these insults are often written off as playful male banter from the frat house. Repeated use of these taunts tends to make them allowable as part of the corporate culture. Sadly, when women hear them over time, they often begin to believe them.

- **Curb the interruptions and credit grabs.** Have you ever been interrupted by a man in a meeting? Or put an idea on the table only to be ignored? When I mention either of these types of interactions to a roomful of women—anywhere

15 Curt Rice, "How Blind Auditions Help Orchestras to Eliminate Gender Bias," *The Guardian*, October 14, 2013, https://www.theguardian.com/women-in-leadership/2013/oct/14/blind-auditions-orchestras-gender-bias.

in the world—heads nod in understanding. Numerous scientific studies reflect that men interrupt women two to three times more often than women interrupt men. While some interruptions can be a sign of familiarity and lively discourse, often they are meant as subtle put-downs or shows of dominance. On the flipside, most women have experienced an instance (or many instances) when they've thrown an idea onto the table for discussion, only to have it greeted with dead silence. Then, when a man repeats the idea as his own, intentionally or not, he is applauded for his creativity and thoughtfulness. Sound familiar? It's not that we can't handle this, but over time, it teaches women that they might as well not bother, that their ideas are not going to be heard, and they simply give up—often without even realizing it. Point out this discrepancy with humor, irony, whatever gets the point across.[16]

- **Take a page from the female US senators.** To remedy the undermining situations above, and to create strength and support among the women in your life, try the strategy called "amplification," which the vastly outnumbered women senators employ in Washington. One way female senators combat undermining is to intentionally repeat an idea put forward by a female colleague and

16 Alice Robb, "Why Men Are Prone to Interrupting Women," *The New York Times*, March 19, 2015, http://nytlive.nytimes.com/womenintheworld/2015/03/19/google-chief-blasted-for-repeatedly-interrupting-female-government-official/.

credit it to that colleague, giving them both the authorship and the floor. It's a brilliant and elegantly simple strategy, but you have to practice it consciously—the occasional happenstance won't have the intended effect. If you face either of these "outshouted" issues, clue in your female colleagues and start amplifying.

- **Lean *on* your male counterparts.** While *leaning in*, the phrase coined by Facebook's Sheryl Sandberg for women owning their power, is a beautiful thing, I actually think it's even more important to *lean on*. That is, to discuss these issues with your male counterparts whenever the opportunity presents itself. If it *doesn't* present itself, make it a point to share your feelings about being passed over for a promotion when you were the most qualified, inequities in your company's hiring practices, or the insults and slights you receive from male peers, from comments on your looks to taunts about your work. It's hard to be the sole woman lodging these complaints, so get some support from others and state your case, factually and unemotionally. (God forbid you come across as an overly emotional female, right?)

An additional note for the men who already lead or support female coworkers. Just do this one simple thing: ask women, in a genuine manner, about the experiences they are having in the workplace. Most women do not want to tell you the truth—they don't want to become the flag bearers for women's issues in your company. They believe it will hurt their careers. They want to be seen as winners, not whiners, and they want to be recognized as great employees and leaders. That said, men, if you ask, I promise the women in your employ will happily share their experiences with you so you can help them close the gender gap.

SHIFTING THE GOLDBERG PARADIGM

Another frustrating, but common, workplace bias is that women are generally considered incompetent until proven competent, while men are thought of as competent until proven otherwise. When a woman makes senior leadership level, many people think that she got lucky, went to the right school, or was friends with the boss. If she fails, it's simply proof of her incompetence. On the other hand, if a man succeeds, it's because of his competence. And if he fails, it's office politics or a scandal, which men can write off (or laugh off) much more easily than a woman can. It's not fair, but it's a reality.

To make matters worse, women can be just as hard on other women as men are. In an experiment dubbed the *Goldberg Paradigm* after the sociologist who created it, researchers asked a group of men and women to evaluate an article or speech supposedly penned by a man. Then they asked a similar group of men and women to judge the same work product, only this time it was presented as having been authored by a woman. Now replicated many times in countries all over the world, men and women routinely judge the work assumed to be written by the woman as far less effective and the woman herself as far less likeable.

While the original study is now nearly thirty years old, at nearly every women's leadership forum I address, women still complain of other women being their harshest critics. My personal theory, and one that is often echoed by other female leaders, is that women have often endured such a struggle to ascend the ladder, they're disinclined to help other women working their way up. Rather, those already in leadership positions feel that more-junior women need to "pay their dues." Instead, women leaders could look at themselves as role models, translating their struggles into strategies (though not a lessening of standards) and coaching other women to succeed as they did.[17]

As leaders, we can't ignore corporate regulations or hiring practices, but we can be far more mindful of these unconscious biases and take preventive action accordingly. While it will be a wonderful day when men take these matters to heart as much as women do, why wait for that time to come when we can make changes on our own that benefit ourselves and other working women?

HOPEFUL HABITS

KEY TAKEAWAY #7

Despite an increase in career advancement for women pro-

---

17 Nicholas Kristof, "When Women Rule," *The New York Times*, February 10, 2008, http://www.nytimes.com/2008/02/10/opinion/10kristof.html.

fessionals over the past twenty years, progress has been slow, and subconscious gender biases are a major factor. We all experience prejudice and bias, based largely on our culture, education, and personal history. It's our job as emerging and established leaders to level the playing field in terms of recruitment, management, and advancement.

HOPEFUL BELIEF #7

Get a gut check on your strengths and weaknesses so you'll have the confidence—and objective data—to defeat, or at least lessen, gender bias and inequality when you encounter them. Do a self-inventory of what you consider your biggest assets as well as your most pressing areas for improvement. Now, see if you can identify your own biases about women in the workplace and gender equality.

HOPEFUL BEHAVIOR #7

Next, ask five trusted colleagues to provide three descriptive words or phrases in answer to the questions: "What do you think are my three greatest strengths?" and "What do you think are three areas where I could improve my performance?" Reconcile the feedback with how you feel about your own work, making sure not to downplay your accomplishments. Decide which improvement you want to tackle first, and get going!

CHAPTER 8

THE GEN BLEND

Generational Perspectives from Gen Z to Traditionalists

"That which seems the height of absurdity in one generation often becomes the height of wisdom in another."
—*Adlai Stevenson*

It was called the most heartbreaking photo of 2015. The boy's name was Alan Kurdi, and he was just three years old when his body washed up on a beach in Greece. His family was fleeing Syria with hopes of traveling to Europe and then on to Canada when the small inflatable dinghy in which they were traveling capsized just a few minutes into their over-water journey. Alan, his older brother Ghalib, and his mother Rihanna died, like the more than five thousand refugees who have perished in the past two years seeking safety outside their home countries.[1][2]

That image, taken by Turkish photographer Nilüfer Demir, quickly went viral, becoming a symbol of all the children who had lost their lives in migration attempts. Like millions of other people, college student Angela Luna couldn't get the photo of the little boy, still in his sneakers as the waves lapped around him, out of her head. But unlike many people, she decided to do something about it. Three weeks into her final project at Parsons School of Design in New York City, she scratched her plans to create a couture evening gown line. Instead, Angela decided to create "functional fashion," clothes that would aid refugees by converting into flotation devices, backpacks, bedrolls, and even tents.

In her TED Talk at Covent Garden, Angela—wearing a t-shirt emblazoned *Decent Human*—confessed that at the time, she had no idea how she was going to achieve her goal. But as she began talking to humanitarian workers and reading interviews with refugees, a vision started to emerge. Although she had considered changing her major to political science, advisors from the nonprofit world encouraged her to stay in the lucrative $1.2 trillion fashion industry. She could tap into the cash flow while designing

1   Bryan Walsh, "Alan Kurdi's Story: Behind The Most Heartbreaking Photo of 2015," *TIME*, December 29, 2015, http://time.com/4162306/alan-kurdi-syria-drowned-boy-refugee-crisis/.
2   Ben Quinn, "Migrant Death Toll Passes 5,000 after Two Boats Capsize off Italy," *The Guardian*, December 23, 2016, https://www.theguardian.com/world/2016/dec/23/record-migrant-death-toll-two-boats-capsize-italy-un-refugee.

recreational clothing, then modify those garments for refugees. Her plan was to create a business model similar to Toms Shoes with its "buy one, give one" program, donating clothing along with every purchase to those in need.[3][4]

As Angela readily acknowledged in her TED Talk, she doesn't expect to solve the refugee crisis. But she does expect to change the conversation about fashion by creating a humanitarian brand that can bring warmth, comfort, and safety using only sustainable materials and ethical business practices. And she encouraged her TED audience to do their part, too. "Find where your skills are needed," she said. "All it takes is a new approach to an old problem. It sure can make a difference." No wonder she named her company *ADIFF*.

GENERATIONAL SNAPSHOT

Millennials like Angela often get a bad rap for being entitled and lazy, but you can see from her story that those labels don't fit her one bit. As useful as age-based labels can be for looking at broad demographic themes, encapsulating

3 TEDx Talks, *Design Intervention For Global Issues*, YouTube video, TEDxCoventGardenWomen, 2016, https://www.youtube.com/watch?v=t0FljT15Dvs.
4 Cadence Bambenek, "Looking to Help Refugees, This Design Student Created Jackets That Transform into Tents and Sleeping Bags," *Business Insider*, July 11, 2016, http://www.businessinsider.com/angela-luna-designs-jackets-to-help-syrian-refugees-2016-7/#luna-emphasized-that-the-collection-isnt-inspired-by-refugees-but-its-intended-to-help-them-by-looking-at-their-needs-and-trying-to-address-those-through-design.

major world events, and even marketing to different groups of consumers, there is so much individual variation within the categories, the generational labeling can't be taken too literally. Sweeping generalizations can be found as far back as the fifth century BC, when Plato said, "Our youth have an insatiable desire for wealth; they have bad manners and atrocious customs regarding dressing and their hair and what garments or shoes they wear."[5][6]

As Lynne Lancaster, coauthor of *When Generations Collide,* stated, "So much of what is going on in our lives is seen through our own generational lens." In this chapter, we'll take a look at that generational spectrum in the workplace today to see which stereotypes hold water and which we should flush for good. We'll also look at how hopeful each generation is, and get some insights on where we might want to put our own focus today so we can look back with real satisfaction tomorrow. Finally, we'll check out how your generation fits in among the others and how you can blend skills and styles to work together collaboratively.[7]

Let's start by breaking down the generations to see what events shaped their worldviews, what their prevailing

5   Wil Buchanan, "The Younger Generation Has Been Ruining The World Since Forever," *Ambitious,* July 24, 2015, http://ambitious. actthreeassociates.com/the-younger-generation-has-been-ruining -the-world-since-forever/.

6   Mary Meehan, "The Perfect Name For The Next Generation Of Americans," *Forbes,* April 15, 2014, https://www.forbes.com/sites/ marymeehan/2014/04/15/the-perfect-name-for-the-next-genera- tion-of-americans/#b14a5bf34162.

7   Lynne C. Lancaster and David Stillman, *When Generations Collide: Who They Are. Why They Clash. How to Solve the Generational Puzzle at Work.* (New York: HarperBusiness, 2002).

attitudes are, and how their group is perceived by others. Most social scientists and business researchers agree that there are four distinct generations in the workplace today, though some identify six groups and most quibble on the exact age breakdown. For our purposes, we'll look at five key generational groups as follows:[8]

- Traditionalists or Silent Generation (born before 1946)
- Baby Boomers (born between 1946 and 1964)
- Gen Xers (born between 1965 and 1976)
- Millennials or Gen Y (born between 1977 and 1995)
- Gen Z (born between approximately 1996 and 2006, though there is not yet a consensus on age range)

TRADITIONALISTS

Traditionalists' values were shaped by the Great Depression, World War II, and the postwar financial and industrial boom, a boom more robust than we've ever seen since. Traditionalists are considered to be among the most loyal employees, possibly because of a deep desire to return to a sense of normalcy after years of political and economic unrest. Savers rather than spenders, this group is thrifty and risk averse when it comes to money, resulting in their

---

8   American Management Association, "The Myth of Generational Differences in the Workplace," *American Management Association*, accessed July 1, 2017, http://www.amanet.org/training/articles/the-myth-of-generational-differences-in-the-workplace.aspx.

being the most affluent elderly population in our country's history. Others generally see them as patriotic and responsible. In the workplace, they tend to be conformist, communicative, and practical.

Key traits: Stable, long-term careers and fiscal responsibility. Stereotypes: Can't learn technology, stuck in their ways.

BABY BOOMERS

The first generation to intentionally prioritize work over their personal lives, Boomers came of age in a period of relative prosperity and growth. Their Traditionalist parents sacrificed a lot to give their kids a better life than they had had. Boomers grew up expecting to go to college, buy a house, and start a family. Their perspective changed with the introduction of television, Vietnam, and the civil rights movement. They became distrustful of government and institutions, prompting them to reject much of what their parents had worked so hard for, particularly in the turbulent 1960s. With the dot-com bust and Great Depression of 2008, many Boomers lost equity in their home and savings. Most Boomers plan to work, at least part-time, longer than they had initially intended, some to make up for the lost savings and others because they can't imagine life in retirement. Known for idealism and individuality, Boomers are also credited as the originators of the "Me Generation."

Key traits: Career focused and competitive. Stereotypes: Materialistic sellouts who weren't around for their kids.

GEN XERS

Gen Xers were born in a time of declining population. Most likely because they grew up in the shadow of the much larger Boomer generation, some people consider them hard to know or understand, hence the X. Author Douglas Coupland coined the Gen X term in his 1991 book entitled *Generation X: Tales for an Accelerated Culture*, and it stuck. Occasionally cynical, always questioning, Xers grew up in a period marked by two-career parents, high divorce rates, institutional fraud, the Iran hostage crisis, and the advent of the AIDS virus. Suspicious of phony values and greedy corporations, Gen Xers wrote the book on work-life balance, unfairly earning them the "slacker" label. Independent and information savvy, Xers are able to adapt to change easily.

Key traits: Flexible and independent. Stereotypes: Cynical slackers.

MILLENNIALS

Coming of age as a new millennium was born, this cohort is the largest since the Baby Boomers. They are the first truly global generation, having grown up with the rapid rise of both technology and terrorism. Despite young lives marked by 9/11, the Columbine shooting, and the Challenger crash, their hovering "helicopter parents" have made them feel cherished and special. Keen to make the planet a better place, Millennials are accustomed to learning and working in diverse teams. Having lived through, and experienced firsthand, substantial gains in education and technology, this generation is the most educated, and many believe the most hopeful, to have come around in many years. Like their Boomer parents, they tend to be hardworking and focused, but unlike the Boomers, they have a deep desire for rapid professional advancement, which has unfairly earned them the "entitled" label.

According to Millennial Jacob Stern, who has worked at a global consulting firm, a major technology company, and is now enrolled in Stanford's Graduate School of Business, "It's not always easy to get young professionals excited about day-to-day tasks when they want to be working on more exciting projects. The best leaders are the ones who can create a strong narrative and really give people a sense of mission. By telling a story about how workers are contributing to the overall financial health of their company, or, better yet, how they are contributing to the good of the world, and continually tying work activities back to this narrative—leaders can create a dynamic culture of high performance."

Entitled or purpose driven (or both), it's clear that Millennials will have a great deal of power in shaping the future of politics, the environment, as well as our business and social structures.

Key traits: Inclusive and global centric. Stereotypes: Entitled and in need of constant praise.[9][10]

---

9   Lauren M. Troksa, "The Study of Generations: A Timeless Notion within a Contemporary Context" (Undergraduate Honors Thesis, University of Colorado Boulder, 2016), http://scholar.colorado.edu/cgi/viewcontent.cgi?article=2273&context=honr_theses.

10 Robert Tanner, "Understanding and Managing the 4 Generations in the Workplace," *Management Is a Journey*, June 28, 2016,

GEN Z

Just when we thought we had a handle on the Millennial generation, there's a whole new group soon to enter the workforce. The first generation of true digital natives, Gen Z consists of toddlers up to college students, most of whom have never known a world without iPhones, Snapchat, or 9/11. According to Gen Z UCLA student and lifestyle blogger Hannah Payne, "Generation Z takes in information instantaneously and loses interest just as fast." But where their Millennial elders were raised in relative peace and prosperity until terrorism and economic downturn changed their world, Zs have grown up with political and financial insecurity. In terms of sheer size, they are a force to be reckoned with, numbering a million more than the Millennials. Marketers and demographers are already looking at them as the next group of retail disrupters, expecting value, selection, and instantaneous delivery. With their knowledge of social media and desire to be entrepreneurial, Gen Z "thought leaders" (yes, you can be an eighteen-year-old thought leader) are selling their savvy to corporations as brand influencers. While the Gen Z story is still being written, expect this group to be tech savvy and entrepreneurial.

THE MULTIGENERATIONAL MIX AT WORK

Imagine this scene. You've been invited to participate in

https://managementisajourney.com/understanding-and-manag-ing-the-4-generations-in-the-workplace/.

your team's digital marketing and communications brain-storming meeting in the company café. The group consists of several fresh-faced Millennials, a handful of Gen Xers, a couple of Traditionalists, several Baby Boomers, and one Gen Z college freshman intern. The team is humming along, throwing ideas across the table, sketching diagrams on the whiteboard, and challenging each other with probing questions. Is it time to overhaul the website, rebrand the blog, introduce a global intranet?

After homing in on several initiatives, the leader wraps up the meeting, handing out assignments and asking for volunteers to take on next steps. The key difference between this group and others that you may have been involved in in the past is that this team is led by a twenty-eight-year-old supervisor. Get used to it. As Millennials continue to climb the corporate ladder, more employees will find themselves being managed by younger leaders. According to a study from EY, 62% of full-time Millennial employees manage other people. It's a new responsibility for most of them, as 85% of Millennial managers moved into leadership roles between 2009 and 2014. Expect it to increase significantly as the workforce grows to nearly half Millennials (46%) by the year 2020.[11]

As Millennials begin to climb the corporate ladder, insisting on work-life balance and purposeful work along

---

11 EY, "Global Generations: A Global Study on Work-Life Challenges across Generations" (EY, 2015), http://www.ey.com/Publication/vwLUAssets/EY-global-generations-a-global-study-on-work-life-challenges-across-generations/$FILE/EY-global-generations-a-global-study-on-work-life-challenges-across-generations.pdf.

the way, the Gen Z kids are just beginning to venture into the open-plan workplace. If their energy is properly focused, this pragmatic and socially connected group may emerge to become a force more similar to their Traditionalist grand- and great-grandparents than any other group. While some claim they have gnat-like attention spans, the Gen Zers themselves contradict that notion, saying that they're able to sift through huge amounts of information very rapidly since they've grown up with screens in their hands. In fact, screen swiping is fast becoming a child development milestone no less significant than standing, walking, or talking.

Michelle Denogean, chief marketing officer for automotive commerce company Roadster, recently told me about an experience she had with a Gen Z summer intern. "A college freshman inquired about an internship opportunity with our company this past summer. I wasn't sure what to expect from an eighteen-year-old, but this young man was turning out data analysis and insights at a manager level within the first few weeks of the job. We have already discussed a role for him once he graduates."

What can you as an employee, or an emerging or established leader, do to help grease the wheels of your multigenerational machine so it can function optimally? Check out these *Dos* and *Don'ts* to see what might work best for your team and organization.

DO

- **Know the demographics.** While you should discourage yourself and others from buying into the negative generational stereotypes, it's important to understand the historically significant themes and prevailing mindsets that helped shape people in each age group. Knowing that Gen Xers grew up working solo while Millennials have learned to thrive in groups may not determine your management style, but it can help inform how you structure and communicate with your different team members.

- **Adapt to your team, don't expect them to adapt to you.** While it might be nice if your multigenerational employees would adapt to your style, it's probably more realistic for you to learn to adapt to *them*. While Traditionalists may prefer more in-person communication and training, Millennials might respond better to computer-based training and text communication. Do what works for your workers.

- **Conduct regular engagement surveys**. Don't try to guess what people are thinking. Conduct surveys to get a handle on what's working for your team, and what's not. Have an open-door policy or, better yet, set regular in-office hours so people know there's a window when they'll have access to you.

- **Experiment with mixed-age teams**. Consider mixing up your team. You might also want to try some reverse-age mentoring programs where older, more experienced workers partner with younger workers for mutual benefit. For example, more-seasoned employees may have advice on communication and career paths, while the younger staff members might share technology hacks or social media insights.

- **Make every generation feel valued.** No matter a person's age, everyone wants to feel valued and respected. Not everyone will define their needs in exactly the same way, but every human being wants to feel a sense of belonging and acceptance. Get to know your team members' strengths, quirks, and passions if you want an engaged workforce.

DON'T

- **Fall for generational assumptions**. Be aware of the stereotypes and assumptions, but don't let them guide your thinking. Instead, see your employees as individuals and manage accordingly. People appreciate it when you keep a level playing field, so practice objectivity in your recruiting, retention, and promotion policies.
- **Bother with age-based affinity groups**. Age-limited cohorts often reinforce negative stereotypes and occasionally devolve into gripe sessions. Unless your people are begging for them, don't bother. Better to offer affinity groups by discipline, location, or other meaningful criteria.
- **Interact just with your age/peer group.** Even if it's more comfortable to engage with people in your age group, don't limit yourself. Get to know people across the generational spectrum

so you can understand what drives them, and what drives them crazy.

- **Forget that followers want trust, compassion, stability, and hope.** Like we saw in chapter five, even if they don't articulate it in these exact words, remember the four key elements that your followers want from you.

HIP HOP, HOPE, AND AGING

Anyone who thinks that hip hop is for the young obviously didn't see the *Hip Hop-eration Crew* compete at the World Hip Hop Dance Championships in Las Vegas. Wearing oversized tees, baggy shorts, neon-colored socks, and Converse high tops, the group of nonagenarians hit the stage to roaring applause. If anyone in the crowd had any preconceptions about what a hip hop troupe looked like, they were completely shattered that day.

The *Hip Hop-eration Crew* (named in honor of the group's many hip surgeries) was born when a team of young hip hop dancers came to visit a senior home in New Zealand. Intrigued, a group of men and women residents got up to dance. A few competitions later and the *Crew* was traveling half-way around the world with their manager, Billie Jordan. Billie had told them, "You're all going...even if it's in an urn." Fortunately, there were no urns involved when the group of twenty-four seniors put aside walkers and wheelchairs to participate. The *Crew* entertained the huge crowd with an exuberance that belied their chronological ages. And that's not all these energetic ninety-somethings accomplished. When most people would be retiring to their rockers, ninety-four-year-old hip hop dancer Kara went backpacking across Asia while eighty-three-year-old Eileen left the group to start her modeling career. While they didn't win the global competition, it was clear who the winners were that day.[12] [13]

FORGET AGING GRACEFULLY; AGE HOPEFULLY

Why is it that some people maintain incredible enthusiasm well into their senior years, while others seem to fade prematurely? My mother Barbara has been a bundle of energy her entire life, learning to fly a plane in her twenties, play golf in her thirties, and race sailboats in her sixties, all while working in healthcare. Now ninety-six years old, she still takes a daily walk unaided, is a voracious reader, and occasionally contemplates writing a book about what ninety-year-olds could be doing with their remaining time.

To make sure she was getting the best care, I consulted former client Anne Ellett, a certified nurse practitioner and expert in dementia and Alzheimer's. Anne founded consultancy Memory Care Support as a resource for family caregivers and care communities. With her extensive background in senior housing and dementia care, Anne's professional expertise includes the establishment of protocols for the management of diseases of the frail elderly,

---

12 LasVegasSun, *Hip Op-Eration*, YouTube video, 2013, https://www.youtube.com/watch?v=GAKEwkhlB_M.

13 The Hip Op-eration Foundation, "The Hip Op-Eration Crew," *The Hip Op-Eration Crew*, accessed July 1, 2017, http://www.hipop-eration.com.

research in the field of dementia, case management of homebound seniors, and supervision of care for patients living in skilled nursing facilities.

When I asked Anne what she'd learned about hope from her years working with seniors, she told me, "I think people are much more hopeful as they age. Many tap into a kind of resiliency where they find themselves less restricted by workplace rules and societal norms. I see people at eighty or ninety exploring new things they've always wanted to try."

Yet, seniors face generational stereotypes just like any age group. Most common is that younger people often focus on their elders' deficiencies, skills they've lost, or limitations they face. We see someone who appears to be frail or has gray hair, and we instantly think about all the things they *can't* do. Instead, Anne advises, shift your perspective to what people *can* do or what they might be able to do with a little assistance.

Just like *Hip Hop-eration* and the young people who inspired them to dance, Anne sees great value in transgenerational connections. She's been pleased to witness the introduction of "learning academies," where older adults help kids with homework and school projects, which she views as extremely beneficial for both age groups. The youngsters get the attention and help they need, and the seniors get the opportunity to share their experience and talents.

"When we stop referring to older people by their diagnoses, the limitations are gone," Anne commented. "Find out what people are great at and what gives them joy. I've seen seniors try everything from storytelling to theater to poetry slams. At this stage of life, seniors have nothing to prove to anyone."

LIGHTING THE WAY

At senior community Starrett Lodge in New South Wales, Australia, Care Service Manager Colin McDonnell has infused hopefulness into the daily life of the residents. Or, as he is careful to call them, "participants, not recipients, of care." Starting with simple changes like opening drapes and adding more furniture and activity spaces outside, Colin introduced more light into the facility, which he found immediately helped with depression, agitation, and sleeping patterns, and also gave the care staff more locations for activities. People began to migrate toward the light, spending more time outdoors interacting with nature and each other. Before long, residents were happier, friendlier, and many of their physical symptoms began to decrease.

Always striving to engage residents in meaningful projects, the Lodge's activities director, Vicki Sanchez, encouraged them to take part in a memory activity, asking them about their early lives and writing down stories for them. That exercise eventually turned into a book of short stories coauthored by the residents called *The Lives We Lived*. The seniors were able to recall events from high school, the Depression, and World War II, and became much closer to each other as they shared their stories. Not only did they write the book, they published and launched it, right down to holding book signings for friends and relatives.

Karaoke night, petting zoos, and family days are all part of the mix as well. Interestingly, even those with dementia instinctively remember how to hold a baby with its head supported or to remove hot coffee when there are young children nearby. As sociologist Cathy Greenblatt, who works with Starrett Lodge, stated, "They are capable of doing a great deal when their self-confidence is renewed."

Proving that you're never too old to try something new, the Starrett seniors decided to start a group bucket list—literally. Each week, they draw one name out of a bucket and fulfil that person's wish. On her turn, one woman wanted to take a friend out for a "posh lunch." The staff ordered a stretch limo and corsages and sent the ladies off for a beautiful seaside lunch, including a "few nips." Others went on helicopter rides, visited vineyards, or went deep sea fishing. A committee of seniors runs the bucket list activities, even finding creative ways to pay for their own outings.

But perhaps the most ambitious—and riskiest—bucket activity to date has been eighty-six-year-old Allen Rigby's skydiving adventure. Although his family was not in favor of his plan, Colin convinced them that as long as seniors have good decision-making capacity, they should be able to make their own choices, even risky ones. Coincidentally, that's the same conclusion I came to when my son Zack wanted to skydive when he turned eighteen. Like Allen's family, I wasn't too keen on the idea, but recognizing that Zack was officially an adult, my birthday gift to him was a skydiving lesson and a tandem jump with an instructor (thankfully required for first-time skydivers).

Though they were eighteen and eighty-six, I think Zack and Allen may have had very similar experiences. As Allen summed it up, "The first twenty feet I felt numb, then I soared. I felt ageless."[14] [15] [16]

HEALTHY LIFE EXPECTANCY

With exceptional care facilities like Starrett Lodge and compassionate and knowledgeable experts like Anne Ellett to guide us, we have a much greater chance of living a happier, healthier, and more hopeful life in our older years. Curious about longevity around the globe, as well as my own life expectancy, I consulted the Blue Zones project. Explorer, author, and educator Dan Buettner teamed up with National Geographic demographers to locate the world's longest-living people and figure out what gave them not only their longevity but their youthful spirit. They identified five geographical locations with the greatest proportions of people who lived to age one hundred or more: the highlands of inner Sardinia; the Aegean Island of Ikaria, Greece; Nicoya Peninsula in Costa Rica; Loma Linda, California (home to a large group of Seventh-day Adventists); and Okinawa, Japan.

From there, Buettner and a team of medical research-

---

14 Uniting, *Finding the Why; Enabling Active Participation in Life in Aged Care*, 2014, https://www.youtube.com/watch?v=hZN1CyEiFNM.

15 Australian Aged Care Quality Agency, "Bucket List Program," *Australian Aged Care Quality Agency*, accessed July 1, 2017, https://www.aacqa.gov.au/providers/promoting-quality/better-practice-awards/2014-better-practice-award-winners/bucket-list-program.

16 Memory Care Support, "Memory Care Support," *Memory Care Support*, accessed July 1, 2017, https://memorycaresupport.com.

ers, epidemiologists, and anthropologists determined the common denominators among these geographically diverse peoples. Buettner calls their findings The Power 9®. To give you some context, the average life expectancy in the United States for someone born today is 78.2 years. When I took the Blue Zones Test, I discovered that my *healthy life expectancy* is 88.2 years, my *actual life expectancy* is 95.5 years, and my *potential life expectancy*—if I make a few changes—is 97.8 years. To find out what I—or you—could be doing differently, I checked out Buettner's Power 9® list, which I've paraphrased below. You can find the entire list at BlueZones.com.[17][18]

1. ***Move naturally.*** Forget the gym and throw out your weed-whacker. Do house and garden work under your own steam and reap the physical rewards.

2. ***Purpose.*** As we've discussed throughout this book, having a deep sense of purpose gives you something to live for, potentially adding seven years to your life.

3. ***De-stress.*** Stress leads to chronic inflammation and other age-related diseases. Find routines and rituals like the Blue Zone folks, from prayer to naps to happy hour.

4. ***Stop eating when you're 80% full.*** Okinawans

17 Dan Buettner, "Power 9," *Blue Zones*, November 10, 2016, https://bluezones.com/2016/11/power-9/.

18 Dan Buettner, *The Blue Zones: Lessons for Living Longer From the People Who've Lived the Longest* (Washington, DC: National Geographic Society, 2008).

recite a Confucian saying before meals to remind them to stop eating when they are 80% full. Blue Zone seniors eat their biggest meal in the morning and their smallest in the early evening, eating nothing after that.

5. *Be plant centric.* Beans, including fava, lentils, black, and soy, are the number one choice among centenarians. They favor vegetables in general, typically eating only five portions of meat per month. That's less than many of us eat in a week.

6. *Wine.* Here's some good news. People in Blue Zones drink moderately, but regularly. One or two glasses of wine per day maximum is suggested, preferably taken with meals and friends.

7. *Practice your faith.* Almost all of the centenarians belong to a faith-based community of some sort. You can add 4-14 years to your life by attending a weekly service. It doesn't much matter, apparently, what the denomination is.

8. *Family first.* Living with or near loved ones and relatives can add years to your life. Interestingly, having elders living with you also reduces disease and mortality rates for kids in the home, too. Commit to a life partner and you can add three years to your expectancy.

9. *Choose your tribe carefully.* Supportive social groups, whether friends or family, that reinforce healthy habits can also add years to your life. Research, such as the *Framingham Study*, has shown that both healthy and unhealthy behav-

iors are contagious, so choose carefully.[19] The Okinawans select groups of five friends, called "moais," that commit to support each other for life. How's that for an accountability group?

HOPEFUL HABITS

KEY TAKEAWAY #8

While it's convenient to categorize people in terms of generational frameworks, it can often lead to false stereotypes and restrictions. Instead, when we look past the clichés and see people as individuals, we get a much better sense of their unique gifts and challenges, hopes and dreams.

HOPEFUL BELIEF #8

Think about the people you know from each of the generational groups outlined above—Traditionalists, Baby Boomers, Gen Xers, Millennials, and Gen Z. Are there stereotypes that you assign to these individuals just by virtue of their age group? What are the stereotypes you hold? How accurate do you think they are? Now, consider your own generational cohort. What stereotypes do people hold about you and your generational counterparts? Are any of them true? If not, how do you challenge them?

---

19 Framingham Heart Study, "History of the Framingham Heart Study," *Framingham Heart Study*, accessed July 1, 2017, https://www.framinghamheartstudy.org/about-fhs/history.php.

HOPEFUL BEHAVIOR #8

Choose someone from another generation that you can partner with to exchange knowledge and expertise. If you're a Millennial, what might you hope to learn from a Traditionalist or Boomer? Conversely, if you're a Boomer, what insights or information could a Gen Xer or Millennial share that would be helpful to your growth? Now, go have the conversation with that person to structure a satisfying cross-generational partnership. If you have a number of close relationships, consider modeling the Okinawan "moais," finding 3-5 people who will all agree to help each other by sharing positive beliefs, skills, support, and feedback.

In the next chapter, we'll see how people who face extreme challenges keep hope alive.

CHAPTER 9

RADICAL HOPEFULNESS

Coping with the Extreme Challenges of Health, Homelessness, and Mental Illness

"Hope is the medicine of the soul."
—Cosette Leary

My brother Cameron is mentally ill. He also holds a master's degree, was an adjunct English professor for twenty-six years, and has published an English Comp textbook and eight novels. Although he has never let his dual diagnoses of schizophrenia and bipolar disorder define him, they have most certainly shaped his life.

Cam's first psychotic break came around the age of fifteen, with another half-dozen serious psychoses to follow over the next forty years. The last one, the worst of all, lasted nearly a year, during which Cameron ended up in jail for trespassing. It was months before we found him—he'd traveled to another state and ended up in custody when he couldn't pay the cab driver. Although all the charges were eventually dropped, by then he'd lost his car, his house, and his job. He also lost most of his friends during his long absence, some of whom he's yet to locate. Despite it all, Cameron says he's eager to reinvent himself, as he has done in the past, with his life growing deeper and richer with each transformation.

In this chapter, you'll meet some incredibly brave people who, like my brother, have dealt with the extreme challenges of failing health, chronic homelessness, and crippling mental illness. Yet, they all have one thing in common: even in the throes of tragic circumstances, they believe that hope can open the door to a better life. As psychologist Dr. Barbara Fredrickson says in her book *Positivity: Top-Notch Research Reveals the Upward Spiral That Will Change Your Life*, "Deep within the core of hope is the belief that things can change. No matter how awful or uncertain they are at the moment, things can turn out better. Possibilities exist. Hope sustains you. It motivates you to tap into your own capabilities and inventiveness to turn things around. It inspires you to plan for a better future."[1]

---

1 Barbara L. Fredrickson, *Positivity: Top-Notch Research Reveals the Upward Spiral That Will Change Your Life* (New York: Three Rivers Press, 2009).

THE EMOTIONAL AND ECONOMIC TOLL OF MENTAL ILLNESS

While most of us assume that mental illness will never touch our lives, psychological disorders are far more prevalent than many people realize. The most common ailments are mood disorders like depression (with more than 350 million sufferers worldwide), bipolar disorder, and dysthymia (low-grade depression). Anxiety disorders include generalized anxiety, social phobia, agoraphobia, and obsessive-compulsive disorder. Substance abuse and impulse control disorders, such ADHD (attention deficit/hyperactivity disorder), like other mental illnesses, are on the rise.

To put things in perspective, here are some of the more eye-opening statistics from the World Health Organization and the National Alliance on Mental Illness:[2][3]

- 1 in 5 adults in the US suffers from mental illness every year
- 1 in 25 adults in the US suffers from a mental illness so severe that it limits one or more major life activities
- Of the 20.2 million people in the US who have

---

2   NAMI, "Mental Health By The Numbers," *NAMI*, accessed July 1, 2017, https://www.nami.org/Learn-More/Mental-Health-By-the-Numbers#sthash.KiuKpUfm.dpuf.

3   The Jason Foundation, "Facts & Stats," *The Jason Foundation*, accessed July 1, 2017, http://jasonfoundation.com/youth-suicide/facts-stats/.

experienced a substance abuse problem, half of
them also have a mental disorder
- 26% of people living in homeless shelters suffer
from a mental illness
- An estimated 18-22 veterans die by suicide
each day
- More teenagers and young adults die from
suicide than from cancer, heart disease, AIDS,
birth defects, stroke, pneumonia, influenza, and
chronic lung disease *combined.*

While we may never be able to calculate the toll of
the human suffering of the mentally ill and the friends,
family members, and colleagues who care about them, it's
a bit easier to calculate the economic toll. According to the
American Psychiatric Association, the cost of treating and
managing mental illness in the US is approximately $55
billion per year. But this doesn't address the overall societal
costs. Factoring in lost or reduced earning power, decreased
taxes, and the cost of accidents and social welfare programs,
the indirect costs of mental illness are estimated at $273
billion per year.

Yet with few resources available for those afflicted and
a society that some believe is lacking in compassion, many
of the half-million people with severe mental illnesses in
the United States end up in emergency rooms, jail, or on
the street every year. As Representative Tim Murphy, a
Republican from Pennsylvania who also happens to be a
PhD psychologist and advocate for the rights of the mentally ill, stated, "We have replaced the hospital bed with the

jail cell, the homeless shelter, and the coffin. How is that compassionate?"

The data reinforces the relevance of Dr. Murphy's pointed question. While nearly 60% of adults believe that people are generally sympathetic toward the mentally ill, only 25% of adults with mental health problems actually believe that others are caring or sympathetic toward them. Cameron has likened this startling lack of compassion—or worse, people overtly taking advantage of the mentally ill—to "buzzards picking us clean."

Most healthcare professionals consider the lack of resources for this fragile population a man-made problem. States have been cutting the number of hospital beds earmarked for the mentally ill for decades. Some of the first cuts came during the Reaganomics era, with the worst coming as a result of the Great Depression, with states reducing their mental health services budgets by approximately $5 billion from 2009 to 2012. The federal government has also made its cuts, eliminating 4,500, or 10%, of public psychiatric hospital beds over the past decade.

What happens to this vulnerable population? Some mentally ill people, like Cameron, can fall back on family for support and sustenance. Others aren't so lucky. Only 40% of adults with severe mental problems, such as schizophrenia and bipolar disorder, received treatment, according to the 2012 National Survey on Drug Use and Health. The other 60% of adults with any type of mental illness went untreated.[4]

---

4   Liz Szabo, "Cost of Not Caring: Nowhere to Go," *USA Today*, accessed July 1, 2017, https://www.usatoday.com/story/news/nation/2014/05/12/mental-health-system-crisis/7746535/.

You may disagree with my assessment or feel that the problem is just too big for any one person to make a difference. And that's okay. But one of the tenets of hope theory is that *true hope* looks at problems and pitfalls straight on, without shying away from some of the uglier truths we'd be much more comfortable ignoring—like that person panhandling on the street corner. Or maybe you've lived, or are living, the caregiving experience and know how hard it is to navigate a city street with a wheelchair-bound family member, or to find low-income housing for a friend on disability. In this chapter, we'll look at some practical ways you can make a difference, no matter what side of the fence you're on.

WARNING SIGNS

While it can be hard to tell if someone has a serious mental problem, especially if you're not a trained healthcare clinician, there are some warning signs. If you believe someone may be a danger to himself or another, call 911 or an emergency mental health hotline in your area immediately. Ask to speak to a mental health professional and be prepared to describe the behaviors that prompted your call.

Changes in emotions or actions, especially sudden ones, can be an indication that your loved one needs assessment and support. Look for the following signs in adults and adolescents:

- Confusion
- Depression, sadness, or irritability
- Extreme high and low moods

- Withdrawal from normally pleasurable social activities
- Changes in eating and sleeping
- Auditory or visual hallucinations
- Strange or paranoid thoughts or delusions
- Anger or excessive fear
- Substance abuse or self-medication
- Suicidal thoughts

HOPING AND COPING

It takes a true leadership mindset to recognize the deep roots of these problems and still want to be part of their solution. While the challenge may seem insurmountable, there are things that we, as individuals, can do to help. You can start by recognizing that mental illness is a disease just like cancer or diabetes. It calls for understanding and compassion, and that includes for yourself as a friend or family member. Cut yourself some slack and remember that most mental illnesses have a biological basis. Bad parenting or poverty rarely cause these illnesses, though they can exacerbate them. Here are some tips to help you cope:

- *Acknowledge your feelings.* Whether you're feeling anger, shame, or guilt about the illness, realize that many people in your situation experience those emotions. You may find yourself worrying about the stigma, ignoring the warning signs, or blaming yourself for causing the illness. Accept those feelings as normal, get educated, and open the lines of communication with others who can help.

- *Get educated about the illness and treatment options.* Knowledge is power, so start learning about your loved one's illness, its symptoms, and available treatment options. Without a deep understanding of how the illness presents itself in its earliest stages, it's hard for people to appreciate the severity of the symptoms, and instead, they wish that their loved one would "snap out of it" or "get their mind off it." It doesn't work that way. There has been plenty of research, however, that demonstrates that when the family is educated and involved in the treatment process, there is often a reduction in symptoms, hospitalizations, and relapses.

- *Seek out a network of support and services.* Start with a family physician or other professional whose opinion you trust to begin to build a caring and supportive network. You may need a general practitioner or internist, psychiatrist, therapist, and possibly others on the team, depending on the illness. Mental illness is the number one factor in disability, so explore medical and disability insurance, food stamps, or anything else that is available to the patient. The National Alliance on Mental Health (nami.org) and Mental Health America (mentalhealthamerica.net) offer education, resources, and classes for individuals and families. As an advocate for a loved one who is an adult, you may want to have him or her sign a HIPAA waiver (that's the legislation that safeguards medical information) so you can communicate regularly with the treatment team.[56]

- *Set realistic expectations.* Mental illness can be highly individualized and unpredictable, so make sure your expectations about symptoms, treatment, and ongoing care are realistic. Recognize that there will be ups and downs, successes and setbacks, and flow with them as well as you can. If your loved one is an adult, allow him or her to have some control in the treatment process. For example, if they can set a schedule for taking their medication and stick to it, let them. On the other hand, some people try to bounce back quickly into "normal life," not wanting to miss more school or work. Keep a watchful eye and get help if you think they're taking on too much too fast. Be mindful that mental illness robs people of their autonomy and dignity, so remain respectful even while you're being vigilant.

- *Take care of yourself.* Mental illness brings not only treatment challenges, but intense emotions. Be sure to take care of yourself while you're caring for someone with a mental illness. Get as much rest, nutritious food, and exercise as possible. You may want to seek out a therapist for yourself, separate from your loved one's care team, to support you in handling both the logistics and emotions you're facing. Most of all, keep in mind that with

5 NAMI, accessed July 1, 2017, https://www.nami.org/#.
6 Mental Health America, "Mental Health America," *Mental Health America*, accessed July 1, 2017, http://www.mentalhealthamerica.net.

proper treatment, many people with mental health challenges do return to a productive and satisfying life. So, keep putting quarters in your own hope machine—they add up.

- *Jump into political action.* In this era of social service cutbacks, it's more important than ever that we lobby our politicians to ensure that the mentally challenged receive the kind of care they need. Too often the ill person's decreased earning power, combined with the need for increased doctor's visits, medications, and hospitalizations, can cause intense economic stress on them and their families. Know how your governor, senator, and representatives stand on the issues and contact them by phone or email to insist on help for the mentally ill. Check out www.house.gov and www.senate.gov for information.

- *Keep hope alive.* Show your loved one that you have faith in a better future by remaining as hopeful as you possibly can. Talk about the future, including them in your vision. Ask for their thoughts about their future, even if it's only for the week ahead. Your attitude alone can help them maintain a positive mindset, knowing that despite the challenges, they will get better.

WHEN HEALTH FAILS

You often hear people say, "If you have your health, you have everything." I'm not so sure about that, just look at some of the *heroes of hope* I mentioned earlier, like Helen Keller and Stephen Hawking. Both had multiple disabilities, yet were still able to make enormous accomplishments.

There are role models for keeping hope alive much closer to home, however. One of them is tax-attorney-turned-energy-healer Belinda Phillips, who I met when she contacted me for help after reading my book *You Unstuck*. "My situation is a little different than most," she told me. After years of coaching, I thought I had seen it all, but Belinda was right.

I was waiting to finally meet her in person in a coffee house in Manhattan Beach when I suddenly heard this loud vocalizing, like a child singing a nonsense song, but in a deeper voice. In strolled a lovely fortyish woman, who I recognized as Belinda, pushing what looked like an adult-sized stroller with her daughter seated in it, making happy noises at the top of her lungs. They were followed by Belinda's other daughter, her adult brother, and her mom.

When she steered her little family parade toward my table, I saw what Belinda was dealing with on a regular basis. Her younger daughter, Marlee, has juvenile diabetes and tuberous sclerosis complex (TSC), a rare chromosomal disease that causes tumors in the internal organs as well as seizures and developmental delays. Her older daughter, Alyssa, who holds a master's degree from Columbia and works as a special education teacher, has an executive and central auditory processing disorder, which makes it challenging for her to take in new information. Belinda's brother is schizophrenic, like my brother Cameron. And her mother, like mine, is a bit too senior to help with the heavy lifting of life, let alone disabilities.

As Belinda's family descended on the coffee shop, heads turned in curiosity. Belinda didn't bat an eye. She gave Marlee her insulin and sent the whole group out for a beach walk so she and I could get better acquainted. I looked at her in awe, this gorgeous woman in her pretty summer dress, hair blown straight and shiny, a touch of gloss on her lips, looking like she'd just stepped out of her office for lunch instead of spending her vacation caring for her entire family.

A lifelong student of human behavior, Belinda had given up her law career so she could care for Marlee at home, a choice with which her then husband strongly disagreed. Caring for Marlee has not only given her a deep sense of purpose, but a range of expertise in healing modalities. Her experience eventually led Belinda into a new career as a healer, helping people get past obstacles and fears.

"We're addicted to fear as part of our survival instinct," Belinda says. "When we move out of it, it's as if our body says *no* and pulls us back in. It's a chemical reaction, and you have to fight it just like an addiction."

When I asked Belinda how anyone can do that, she had several suggestions. First, find a daily practice of some kind that connects you to something bigger than yourself. It might be something spiritual, like prayer or meditation, but it doesn't have to be. Other alternatives include yoga, journal writing, or qigong, a Chinese practice of movement and breathing. But don't expect any practice to change your life overnight, she cautions, because it can take time to let go of fear and past trauma, until suddenly we realize our energy has gone from feeling like we're slogging through a swamp to feeling effortlessly light and dreamy.

Another habit that Belinda emphasizes in her work is to let go of thinking you can do everything alone. We all need a guide, or better yet, a team. We need to invest in people, financially or otherwise, who make us a priority, just as we make others a priority for us. Find a group, trainer, coach, spiritual partner, or anyone who can give you strength and power. No surprise that Belinda's personal hero is Dr. Viktor Frankl, the Viennese psychiatrist I mentioned earlier—also one of my heroes.

"Noticing and tapping into my magical energy makes me more loving and nurturing," Belinda says. "When I'm in tune with my daily practice, not always easy with the demands on my time, even Marlee is happier and stronger. You don't have to believe in your practice at first, you just have to keep trying it until you find what works for you."

BUBBLES OF CONTENTMENT

Milwaukee resident Eliz Greene had given up hope on having biological children. After numerous attempts with infertility treatment, she and her husband had come to decide that if they never had kids, life would still be okay. But on the day she finally decided to call it quits, Eliz and her husband went to visit a friend with a newborn baby. Holding the baby, her husband suggested they give it one more try. It worked, and Eliz was soon pregnant with twins.

The pregnancy was a difficult one, and Eliz ended up on bed rest in the hospital. She was in preterm labor for nearly three months with regular contractions, just trying to hold on long enough for the babies to develop. After a month of lying on her left side, getting out of bed for bathroom breaks only if she wasn't contracting, Eliz suddenly began to feel ill. She vomited several times, then buzzed for the nurse, thinking she needed antacid for heartburn.

The nurse took one look at Eliz's ashen face and knew it was more than indigestion. As Eliz describes it, she was as lucky as anyone could be who was in cardiac arrest. It was a Sunday, and though the hospital was quiet, her obstetrician was standing at the nurse's station thirty feet away, and a respiratory therapist, as well as a cardiac surgeon and his entire team, were in the hospital. Eliz coded and the team restarted her heart with a defibrillator. Once she was stable, they performed a cardiac catheterization and discovered what had gone wrong. Because of the hormones that soften the tissue for birth, the inside lining of her cardiac artery had peeled away from the outside, leaving an opening like a trap door. That's what had stopped the flow of blood and caused the heart attack. After the catheterization, Eliz was taken to the cardiac operating suite, where her twin girls were born by emergency C-section, followed by major heart surgery.

Eliz's girls were two months premature, but now, sixteen years later, they are healthy and happy. But Eliz still replays that day in her head, especially when someone bemoans yet another birthday. "Better than the alternative," she always tells them, knowing exactly how true that is. Eliz has since become an author, healthy living advocate, and stress management speaker. She has surveyed more than three thousand employees to ascertain what their major work stressors are. Though she's still compiling her extensive research, she is already seeing something of a pattern with key stressors such as uncertain future, negative work environment, and high volume of workload.

She calls these work and life challenges "the swirl," as in all the things that swirl around us and make us feel out of touch with what's truly important. To combat this, Eliz does an exercise with her lecture audiences. Handing out packets of Post-it Notes, she asks everyone to write down everything that's calling for their attention—credit card bills, work, kids' schedules—one challenge per Post-it.

People get a great sense of clarity, Eliz reports, when everything is out of their heads and onto the Post-its. From there, she tells her audience they have to pare down their Post-its to only three things, and one of those must be themselves. That leaves only two left over for work, family, fitness, or whatever is most important. Those three circles, she tells them, are their *bubbles of contentment,* where they should be finding the most joy as they focus their time and energy. The rest of the items go back into the swirl. Incredibly liberating!

FROM HOMELESSNESS TO HOPEFULNESS

Although the individual circumstances of homelessness are as complex and varied as the people themselves, below is a snapshot that tells the story of a single night in January 2016 in our country. The Department of Housing and Urban Development (HUD) requires communities to submit "point in time" homelessness data every two years in order to qualify for federal assistance funds. Here's what the most recent data tells us:[7][8]

- **549,928 people** were homeless on a given night in the United States
- Of that number, 194,716 **were people in families**
- **355,212 were individuals**
- On that same night, there were **35,686 unaccompanied homeless youth**, roughly 7% of the total homeless population
- 77,486 or one in five were considered "chronically homeless," defined as someone who has experienced homelessness for a year or longer, or who has experienced at least four episodes of homelessness in the last three years (must be a cumulative of twelve months), and has a disability.

Despite those stunning statistics, there is cause for hope. Between 2015 and 2016, the number of people experiencing homelessness declined in thirty-seven states, with the largest decreases by number of people in Florida (down 2,341), New York (down 1,898), Illinois (down 1,587), Massachusetts (down 1,527), and Nevada (down 1,345). The largest percentage decreases were in North Dakota

---

7 National Alliance to End Homelessness, "Cronically Homeless," *National Alliance to End Homelessness*, accessed July 1, 2017, http://endhomelessness.org/homelessness-in-america/who-experiences-homelessness/chronically-homeless/.

8 Meghan Henry et al., "The 2016 Annual Homeless Assessment Report (AHAR) to Congress" (The U.S. Department of Housing and Urban Development, November 2016), https://www.hudexchange.info/resources/documents/2016-AHAR-Part-1.pdf.

(29%), Vermont (27%), West Virginia (24%), Montana (17%), and Nevada (15%).

BEACONS OF HOPE

To really understand the experience of homelessness, however, you have to meet the people and hear their stories. Which, in itself, is a challenge, because as most homeless people will tell you, they are part of an invisible population. In 2014, the New York City Rescue Mission, a homeless shelter, conducted an experiment dubbed *Make Them Visible*. In it, people disguised themselves as homeless and were filmed walking past their own relatives. Not one of them was noticed by their own family members just a few feet away. Michelle Tolson, director for the shelter at that time, noted, "We don't take a second look."

Cosette Leary, who I met after she took one of my online webinars, refused to be invisible. Even as a single woman on welfare raising young children, she knew her destiny was to lift herself and her kids out of homelessness and poverty. Cosette had been removed from her home at age twelve due to domestic abuse and consequently grew up in a patchwork quilt of foster care, youth shelters, and orphanages. By the time she was twenty-seven, Cosette had four children of her own and was living hand to mouth, picking up shifts as a nurse's aide or daycare worker.

At her lowest points, Cosette told me, she would drag her kids with her into a discount store to look at the picture calendars, hoping she would find one with an image of a lighthouse. "Those lighthouses were like beacons of hope to me, symbols that I would eventually find my way home."

One rainy day in total frustration about how to entertain her kids, Cosette discovered the magic of her public library. While the kids drew or looked at picture books, Cosette discovered rows of business books and journals. Turned on by her newfound love of learning about business, Cosette was fascinated to read a profile about franchising expert Dina Dwyer Owens in *Working Mothers Magazine.* Cosette contacted Dina, and the next thing she knew, she was meeting with her and learning about business, college, and life. Cosette had received her GED (after five tries), but now, with Dina's encouragement, she enrolled in college.

It wasn't easy being a student with four kids and few resources, but Cosette graduated with honors and headed to Washington to take a class at the Brookings Institution, so she "could be like Condaleeza Rice." When her instructors discovered that Cosette had made her way from working a minimum wage job to getting a certificate from Brookings, they connected her with a senator from New York, who gave her an internship in his Harlem district. Now creating a pilot program to guide low-income people out of poverty, Cosette is a beacon of hope for others.

COACHING A NATION

Toronto-born Lia Grimanis is also a survivor of domestic violence. Like Cosette, she left home as a young teen and spent ages 16-19 couch surfing until she discovered the existence of a homeless shelter. As Lia explained to me, "Couch surfing is just as dangerous as living on the streets because you run out of friends very quickly and have to cultivate new ones. Then you find yourself sleeping on a

stranger's couch behind a locked door." Sadly, women fleeing violence often become victims of even greater violence,
as did Lia.

Lia spent the next three years in constant turmoil,
couch surfing then living in the shelter until she was placed
in affordable housing. She was suicidal during much of
that time, literally debating with herself about whether she
wanted to live or die. One day, sitting on her shelter bed,
she not only decided that she wanted to live, but made
herself a promise that she would become so successful that
the media would have to shine a spotlight on her story. Her
ultimate goal was to come back to the homeless shelters
and social programs to tell people that she had made it out
and they could, too.

Despite her tenth-grade education, Lia eventually got
a job selling software and set her sights on becoming one of
the most successful people in the company. In one of those
rare moments of magic, the company hired a coach for Lia,
who inspired her to think big and give back. After that, Lia
was among her company's top three salespeople in Canada
or globally every year.

After becoming a successful businesswoman and
entrepreneur, Lia created the nonprofit foundation Up
With Women to help women and children rebuild their
lives after homelessness. Coaching, which had profoundly
affected Lia's life, is the cornerstone of the program, with
coaches volunteering to coach and mentor one woman
each for an entire year.

As Lia describes Up With Women, "The women who
come to our program have already written half of their success story, which is much more than mere survival. They

grow into leaders because every woman who flees violence or exits poverty becomes a role model for those behind her."

The coaches she partners with the homeless women are integral to their success. All the coaches are on their second or third careers and are committed to helping others. Additionally, the organization has been built by (and for) people who have experienced violence, sexual abuse, mental illness, or homelessness, and who are highly relatable for the women in the program. Finally, every woman who goes through Up With Women's coaching program wants to ensure that no one else has to go through similar hardships. Ego takes a back seat, and the organization takes on a deeper level of purpose and significance. "It's no longer personal," Lia says. "It's about all of us." Indeed.

I live in Los Angeles, where I regularly see homeless people on the street or sidewalks. I asked Lia what we can do, as individuals, when we encounter homeless people in our own cities or neighborhoods. Here are Lia's suggestions:

- Look them in the eye. Don't let homeless people feel invisible.
- If you want to offer money, do. But you can also offer to buy lunch, or stop in at a grocery store or fast food spot and bring a brown bag back to the person in need. Lia often offers to take homeless people to a restaurant for a meal. Most of us would be uncomfortable doing that, but having been in their place, Lia knows that the caring conversation is as nourishing as the food.
- Donate to the services that help the homeless. While your spare change or a bite to eat will

likely be welcomed, organizations that are set up to help the homeless are in a far better position to do good.

- If you've ever been homeless or in poverty, share your story and let the homeless person know that there is hope and help for them.

HOW DO YOU GET TO CARNEGIE HALL?

You know the old joke with its oft-repeated response: practice, practice, practice.

One group got to Carnegie Hall with practice and the help of the Dallas Street Choir. The choir, made up of the city's homeless, was founded in 2014 by conductor and music educator Dr. Jonathan Palant with the tagline: *Homeless, not voiceless.* Although membership has changed over the past few years, there is now a solid contingent of twenty-five core members, some with mental illness and addiction issues, who were among those picked to tour the East Coast.

The sold-out concert on January 25, 2015, was the first time in the 126-year history of the venerable Carnegie Hall that it has hosted a performance by a homeless choir. Discussing their sound, choir director Palant confesses, "We're scrappy. We acknowledge that. But it's unbridled, passionate, filled with love and joy and uniqueness." Just like the singers themselves, no doubt.[9]

---

9 "The Dallas Street Choir Makes Historic Carnegie Hall Debut," Online radio recording, *All Things Considered* (NPR, June 14, 2017), http://www.npr.org/2017/06/14/532959314/the-dallas-street -choir-makes-historic-carnegie-hall-debut.

HOPEFUL HABITS

KEY TAKEAWAY #9

Despite the extreme challenges of failing health, chronic homelessness, and crippling mental illness, there is hope. From recognizing the issue to changing your mindset to creating a support network, life can improve. The remarkable role models cited in this chapter shared some simple things you can do to help.

HOPEFUL BELIEF #9

Imagine a day in your life as a person who is homeless and suffering from poor physical or mental health. Take yourself through the entire day, from waking up on the street or in a shelter to finding food, bathroom facilities, and a place to sleep at night. How would your day be different? What would you miss most? Would you feel ashamed? Frightened? Resigned? Where would you turn for help?

HOPEFUL BEHAVIOR #9

Pick one action you can take that would benefit a member or members of this fragile population. Will you volunteer in a shelter or soup kitchen? Take a homeless person to a coffee shop for lunch? Give some relief to a friend or family member who is a primary caregiver by offering to cook a meal, do the laundry, or sit in for them so they can run errands or take a nap? How will you be a messenger of hope?

In chapter ten, we'll pull everything together so you can create your *True Hope Roadmap,* combining beliefs and behaviors, skills, and support to get you where you want to go next!

CHAPTER 10

YOUR TRUE HOPE ROADMAP

Mastering the Habit Formation Formula

"Action is the foundational key to all success."
—*Pablo Picasso*

Sometimes we're given clues that it's time to make a change. The signs are all there, pointing us in a new direction. All we have to do is take the leap. I was given that kind of cosmic kick in the rear when I was working at Universal. In a very unusual deal, media mogul Barry Diller had purchased part of the television group and rolled it into his existing company. I was being courted for a senior communications position. The new role would have given me some interesting challenges as well as a lot of visibility with media and stakeholders.

I was torn. I'd already been considering leaving the industry to pursue a different career path, though I wasn't quite sure what that was at the time. But being a good corporate citizen—as well as the sole support of my family—I decided to play it out and see what happened. As part of that process, one of my staff members would typically prepare a press release to be disseminated to media should I accept the job. Since my team oversaw press announcements, we went through the standard protocol. Which meant I had to sit for a new headshot, which would accompany the pending release.

My team set up the shoot, my photo was taken, and then I promptly forgot about it. A few days later, I opened a large manila envelope that had been placed in my inbox. There, staring back at me, was an 8x10 black and white proof of my headshot with every flaw on my face circled in red grease pencil. And it didn't stop there. Scribbled in red across my face were noted all the fixes that the photographer was requesting from the re-toucher, a sort of photographic plastic surgery for my poor, put-upon face.

Brighten the red eyes.

Whiten the dull teeth.

Fix the gray hair.

Lose the crow's feet.

Lessen the wrinkles.

Had they been able to remove the thirty pounds I'd gained due to the stress of the job compounded by a failing marriage, I might have been more grateful. As it was, I sat and stared at that photo as the tears began to roll down my cheeks. If I had unexpectedly caught a glimpse of myself in a store window on my worst day, I couldn't have been more shocked. This was what I looked like? This was who I had become? This harried, matronly, chubby-faced woman who had failed utterly at hiding how miserable she was—this was *me*?

I made a decision then and there that things had to change. That *I* had to change. Although I'd come a long way from the girl wrapped in the mink coat, clutching a bottle of brandy, I wondered if this was another kind of stasis in which I'd allowed myself to become trapped. So I set out on a journey to create the next iteration of my personal and professional life. I turned down the communications job, much to the shock of my friends and colleagues, who couldn't believe I was passing on such a fabulous opportunity. And for the next few years, I experimented with everything from producing reality shows to teaching a university entertainment business course to conducting seminars on career change.

Slowly, a path—more purposeful and satisfying than I'd ever thought possible—emerged. Seventeen years later, I've coached hundreds of Fortune 500 leaders and presented keynote addresses from Colombia to Kuwait. I've written six books and traveled the world for both work and pleasure. I've reinvented my relationships with my two wonderful sons, which had been painfully strained through the dark days of my divorce. I live in a beautiful home in Southern California, and I have a significant other whom I love dearly. To suggest that this is a whole new life for me would be a vast understatement.

Though it may be a cliché to say, "If I can do it, you can do it," in this case, it also happens to be true. Fortunately, over the past seventeen years of coaching and consulting,

I've learned what it takes to envision and implement change, both for individuals and organizations. That's what I want to share with you now: how to create a roadmap based on *true hope*. That is, a roadmap based on a soaring image of the best life you can possibly have, yet one that is totally grounded in reality and deeply pragmatic at the same time. If I can shave a few years, or decades, off your learning curve, I will have done my job. So dig in and get ready to pull everything you've learned from this book together into one glorious master plan.

THE HABIT FORMATION FORMULA

Before I show you how to build your roadmap, it's important to look at the facts and fictions about goals and habits. That is, how beliefs become behaviors, and how behaviors become habits. It's a lot easier to follow through with positive actions when they reach *automaticity*, meaning that they become as routine as brushing your teeth or combing your hair. By understanding the science behind habit formation, you'll be better equipped with not only the *why* but also the *how* and *when*.

There's a common misconception that you can form a habit in twenty-one days. Like lots of other urban legends, this one is rooted in a little bit of truth. Dr. Malcom Maltz was a plastic surgeon who wrote the blockbuster self-help book *Psycho-Cybernetics* in 1960. I remember this book vividly, having purchased a copy with my babysitting money when I was a teenager. My dad, a traditional psychiatrist, was not a fan of anything that smacked of self-help—"They're all quacks," he would tell me. So I kept the book hidden under my bed, retrieving it at night to read when everyone was asleep. Dr. Maltz noticed that when he performed plastic surgery on patients, it took most of them approximately twenty-one days to become accustomed to their new nose, chin, or implants. Over the years, his message got twisted and restated by his many fans, among them teachers, coaches, and self-help gurus, who insisted that it took twenty-one days to form a habit.

Not so, confirms further research. One such study in the *British Journal of General Practice* found that it takes most people approximately sixty-six days for a habit to take hold. So if you've been struggling to make your workout, diet, or career plan become habit forming in a mere three weeks, only to discover that it's not happening, it's time to reset your expectations. Habit formation will take you longer than you initially thought—and may be harder than you hoped—but it's absolutely doable. Now that you're armed with a vision and some realistic expectations, which is the very definition of *true hope*, let's look at some of the steps you can take to make sure your goals actually stick.[1]

FOUR STEPS TO HABIT FORMATION

We tend to think of habits as behaviors that get repeated. But, in psychological terms, habits are actions that are automatically triggered in the context of a specific situa-

1 Benjamin Gardner, Phillippa Lally, and Jane Wardle, "Making Health Habitual: The Psychology of 'habit-Formation' and General Practice," *The British Journal of General Practice* 62, no. 605 (December 2012): 664–66, doi:10.3399/bjgp12X659466.

tion—for example, putting on your seatbelt after getting in the car or washing your hands after using the bathroom. *When the action is repeated based on the contextual cue that triggers it, it becomes a habit.*

When I was a kid, people rarely used seatbelts. Changing people's seatbelt-wearing habits required a long-term, multipronged effort including legislation, advertising, and even the cooperation of film and television studios showing the stars buckling up. I was part of the effort to lobby TV producers to portray their lead characters buckling up. The goal wasn't just to educate people about safety, it was to make seatbelt wearing automatic. Now, if you try to back out of your driveway without giving your kids the necessary time to buckle their belts, you're likely to hear them holler. Most people don't even think about it anymore—they just secure the belt. That's *automaticity.*

The beauty of automaticity is twofold. First, the action requires so little thought on your part that your brain is free to focus on other things, like that bike in the driveway, or the truck that's pulling out behind you. Secondly, when your willpower or motivation starts to wane, the habit still sticks because it takes so little effort that it's become reflexive. Further, if you fail to perform the action (take, for example, not wearing your seatbelt or missing your workout), it just feels weird. Eventually, it takes more effort *not* to perform the task you've worked so hard to program into your mind and life.

I've broken down what I consider to be the four essential steps to habit formation. If you approach them in order, one step at a time, forming positive habits will be easier than you think. Step #1 of habit formation is the *selection phase,* where you choose the behavior and the context in which it will be performed. For example, if you've decided you need to incorporate more fruit into your diet, you make it part of your daily breakfast. If you want to make walking a part of your exercise routine, you leave your shoes beside your bed at night and head out every morning at 6:30. When you repeat the behavior in the same context—fruit for breakfast, walking at 6:30—it's more likely to stick.

Step #2 is the *repetition phase*, where you perform the chosen behavior, linked to the appropriate context, over a length of time. For some people, this might be as few as six days (again, let go of the twenty-one-day notion), or it could be as long as nine months before automaticity kicks in. Once the behavior becomes automatic, it's just a matter of keeping it going, especially when your lifestyle or routine changes. Missing the chosen behavior once in a while doesn't seem to affect the overall process of habit formation. So don't give up on the action if your routine gets disrupted—which it inevitably will. Just get right back on the habit horse.

Step #3 is the *expansion phase*, where you increase the intensity, time, or strength of the habit you're forming. For example, say you've started walking (action) at 6:30 each morning (context) for twenty minutes. After a week, add a little bit to the time or intensity. Maybe you increase your twenty minutes to twenty-five, or you add an uphill stretch to your walk. When you ramp up your time, pace, or intensity in small increments, you'll hardly even notice that you've increased the effort needed. Do this for a week, then add on a little more. If it's a strain, back it down to your prior level and work your way up again. The idea is to add micro-increases slowly over time. Trust me, the small wins will add up to big results.

Step #4 is the *automaticity phase*, where the habit has become so routine that you rarely even think about it—you just do it. At this point, you've achieved solid habit strength and the action has become a normal part of your life, requiring very little effort on your part. In case you're wondering, stopping a habit is far more difficult than forming a habit. It's hard to make a habit out of *not* doing something. If you're trying to stop smoking or overeating or overdrinking, I applaud you. But you may want to try forming a new habit that slowly replaces the old one.

A word of caution: variation is the enemy of automaticity. Even though many experts suggest that you "mix it up" to stave off the boredom of repetition, it's actually the repetition—in context—that builds automaticity. So be wary of switching up the context in which you perform the action. Even if your schedule gets hectic or you're traveling, you're still likely to be able to find a piece of fruit for breakfast or take a walk at your usual time. And, as I said before, a miss or two won't affect your overall habit formation, so don't even try to tell yourself you might as well give it up if your routine gets thrown off.

Let's recap the process of habit formation:

1. Choose a *goal* that you'd like to achieve. Make it count. If you don't care about it, you're not likely to stick with it.
2. Select a simple daily *action* that will move you toward your goal.
3. Decide when and where you will practice that

action consistently. This provides the *context* for the action.

4. *Repeat* the action each day.
5. *Expand* the intensity, time, or effort in tiny increments.
6. Keep going until you've achieved *automaticity*. Remember the sixty-six-day rule and cut yourself some slack until it becomes effortless.
7. You've formed a positive habit. Time to celebrate!

HABIT HACKS TO HELP SOLIDIFY GOAL STRENGTH

Life isn't perfect, and routines often fail. Which is why, even if you're using the *Habit Formation Formula* I described above, you'll still need some back-up tools and techniques at the ready. Check out these three habit hacks to help you make your habits meaningful and automatic.

THE IF-THEN PIVOT

James Clear is an author, photographer, and weightlifter. He also happens to be a blogger who writes about goal setting. Given the wide variety of his occupations, it's a good thing that he sets clear objectives and follows through tenaciously. James describes one of the techniques he uses to keep on track as the *if-then method*. James says, "Sometimes you won't be able to implement a new behavior—no matter how perfect your plan. In situations like these, it's great to use the *if-then* version of this strategy."

The way it works is simple. You set your goal (the first step to creating a habit) as described above. But you allow for potential disruption by adding a pivot, like so: if *this* (meaning an obstacle or change in plans) happens, I'll do *this* (replacement behavior) instead. For example, if your boss has scheduled a 7 am meeting that precludes your 6:30 am walk, then you would use the if-then pivot: "If I don't have time for my 6:30 walk, then I'll walk at 7 pm when I get home from work." By planning for the unexpected, you'll always have a workaround at the ready, no matter where you are in the process of habit formation.[2]

TO SHARE OR NOT TO SHARE

Once you've determined a goal that is meaningful to you, do you share it with others or keep it to yourself? It's a personal choice, of course, but there is an argument to be made for both scenarios. In an article published in *Psychological Science*, NYU professor of psychology Dr. Peter Gollwitzer suggests that sharing your goals may actually give you less incentive to accomplish them.

Here's why: when you share what are known as identity goals—that is, ones that express who you are or wish to become—you may unconsciously feel as though you've already planted that perception, or identity, in the minds of others. Consequently, you don't work as hard to achieve

2   James Clear, "Achieve Your Goals: The Simple Trick That Doubles Your Odds of Success," *James Clear*, accessed July 31, 2017, http://jamesclear.com/implementation-intentions.

the actual goal. In Dr. Gollwitzer's study, the research team asked students who had communicated a desire to become career psychologists to list two activities that would help them accomplish that goal. Half of the group who handed in their lists was told that the researchers would read and comment on them. The other half was told that their list would not be read by anyone. In what seems like a counterintuitive result, when asked a week later how much time they had spent on their chosen activities, the group who *did not* share their goals was found to have spent considerably more time on their chosen activities.

The researchers' conclusion was that wanting to create a specific identity (in this case, to become a psychologist) motivated the non-sharers to actually perform their chosen activities. On the other hand, the people who had their activities reviewed by the researchers felt as though they had already fulfilled their desired identity. Therefore, the motivation to work in service of the goal was significantly decreased. To put it simply, by claiming their identity as future psychologists, the sharing group had less to prove.[3]

In my experience coaching individuals and running groups dedicated to goal achievement, I've often found the opposite to be true. I've seen that people who express a specific goal, and then share that goal with people they trust, are much more likely to follow through than those who keep their goals to themselves.

Why? Here are just a few of the reasons:

---

3 Peter M. Gollwitzer et al., "When Intentions Go Public: Does Social Reality Widen the Intention-Behavior Gap?" *Psychological Science* 20, no. 5 (2009): 612–18.

- *Goal Clarity.* By stating your goals out loud to others, you achieve a deeper level of clarity about your goal, including the why, when, and how you plan to make it happen. In addition, as people jump on board to discuss your goal with you, you add nuances that further clarify your goal. Additionally, the person with whom you're sharing may have had a similar experience and could provide insights about what worked, or didn't work, that might be helpful to you.

- *Motivational Metrics.* Like sharing your goals to deepen the clarity, adding specific measurements can help keep you on track. When you start with the assumption that it will take you sixty-six days (or longer) to form a habit, you can break your goal down into chunks and share those milestones with others. With both cheerleaders and challengers on board, you can get the support you need when you hit a snag, as well as the acknowledgement when you hit a target. Either way, the input from others can give you the psychological boost you need to stick with it.

- *Accountability for Action.* When you tell a friend or family member that you plan to lose thirty pounds or take a writing course, you're adding another layer of intentionality, making your goal more real and solid. Plus, the person with whom you've shared is likely to continue asking you about progress. As human beings, we want the support and recognition for our achievements, that psychological pat on the back for staying the course. You can take this one step further and form an accountability group of like-minded, goal-oriented people who come together on a regular basis to share their progress. The goals need not be the same; rather, it's the shared experience of both setbacks and achievement that helps you keep moving forward.

POSITIVELY CONTAGIOUS

Just like yawning, smiling, or laughing, attitudes and behaviors can be contagious. Because human beings are built for survival, we have a primal desire to create strong bonds with others, for protection and for the hunting and gathering of food. It is true, however, that more subtle, emotional responses can be just as contagious. These responses include negative behaviors, such as overeating, overdrinking, or blowing off exercise. If that's how your family or friends roll, you may choose to do the same even though you are well aware that those choices are bad for you and your health.

Similarly, positive behaviors can spread from one individual to another, or through entire groups or organizations. In an experiment at Yale meant to approximate a corporate workplace, two groups were assigned the task of giving employees bonuses. The catch was that they were told to give the largest bonuses possible to a few specific people, yet at the same time ensure that their choices would be fair to the group as a whole. An actor was planted in each group to steer the intentionally contradictory task. One actor was upbeat and enthusiastic in his presentation, while the actor in the other group was negative and unhappy. The first group, with the upbeat actor, came to a conclusion that everyone felt good about, while the other group struggled uncomfortably with the assignment.

Simply by being aware how much our attitudes and actions impact other people, leaders can consciously turn the tide on how their team, if not their entire organization, feels and behaves. Just as in primitive times when tribes looked to their leaders for signals, your employees naturally look to the most powerful players to see what they're feeling, especially in times of uncertainty like mergers or corporate restructures. When you provide positive cues through verbal and nonverbal language, people are likely to follow your lead, which in turn, helps them manage their fears and insecurities so they can do their best work.[4]

CREATING YOUR TRUE HOPE ROADMAP

Now it's time to get down to the exciting job of weaving all this information together so you can create your *True Hope Roadmap*. Remember that *true hope* includes your vision of the future as well as a recognition of the obstacles you might hit along the way. By creating a meaningful vision that moves you deeply, combined with some easy workarounds for the challenges you may face, you'll be uplifted by passion and grounded by pragmatism.

4   Carol Kinsey Goman, "Great Leaders Are Positively Infectious," *Forbes*, July 11, 2012, https://www.forbes.com/sites/carolkinseygoman/2012/07/11/great-leaders-are-positively-infectious/#2f551ed578cc.

CLARIFY YOUR VISION

Let's start with your vision. Think of that as the *why*, or the big-picture ideal for your work and life as well as the value behind it. Next, we'll add goals—that is, the *what*, or action steps. Then we'll establish the context—that's the *when* and *how* that will trigger your actions. Finally, we'll layer in the workarounds to get past the inevitable challenges that will pop up as you move forward.

For starters, clear your mind using whatever practice or technique works best for you, including meditation, writing in a journal, or just sitting quietly so you can let your thoughts flow freely. (If you need more help from me, read my book *Traveling Hopefully*.) Now take a big leap into the future—a decade into the future to be precise. Imagine what your life looks like by asking yourself the questions:

- What do you do for work? What are the environment, team, and tasks like?
- What's happening with your finances? Income? Savings? Retirement or college plans?
- Who's in your life? Significant other? Family? Friends? Colleagues?
- What do you do for fun? How do you spend your leisure time?
- How are your health and self-care? Exercise? Nutrition? Sleep?
- What is your home or living space like?

This is blue-sky time, so jump as far into the future as you can without bogging yourself down with details or negatives like "How will I get there?" or "What skills do I need to make that happen?" or "I don't have a romantic partner." Instead, let your imagination run wild, with no restrictions and no censorship, as you picture your ideal work and life. Take as much time as you need to write out your vision.

SET YOUR GOALS AND CONTEXT

Next, begin to set your specific goals, including the action steps and context for each. This is where you can also begin to think about a logical sequence in which things might unfold. To get started, select one personal goal and one professional goal that align with your vision. You can use my sample list below or choose goals of your own, layering in more action steps after you've mastered the process.

Sample Professional Goals

- Enhance my leadership skills
- Boost my visibility on the job
- Strengthen my personal brand
- Move up to the next level in my organization
- Get a new certification or degree
- Attend a professional conference
- Broaden my network
- Add key staff members to my team
- Find a new role in my company
- Start a business

Sample Personal Goals

- Start a new fitness program

- Spend more time with family
- Get on top of my finances
- Find a romantic partner
- Buy a home
- Travel the world

Okay, let's say you chose *get a new nursing certification* as your professional goal and *find a romantic partner* as your personal goal. Now, let's add a couple of action steps (obviously, there can be more than one step associated with a goal) for each, as well as the context in which you'll take the action. Here's how that might look:

Goal: Get a new nursing certification

- Action/Context – Speak with my supervisor about what certification would be the most relevant for career advancement.
- Action/Context – Register and attend class every Tuesday night from 7-10 pm for six weeks.

That's pretty specific. You've confirmed with a trusted colleague what certification would be most valuable for your professional development. You've located the appropriate course and registered. Now, if it's Tuesday night at 7 pm, you know exactly where you're supposed to be and what you'll be doing. If you need further accountability, put the goal on your calendar, share it with a friend, or get a colleague to join you.

Let's do the same with your personal goal—finding a romantic partner. Again, drill it down to define the associated action or actions.

Goal: Find a romantic partner

- Action/Context – Join a dating site and carve out Thursday evening and Saturday morning for potential coffee dates.
- Action/Context – Tell ten friends you'd appreciate any introductions they can provide.

Again, you've set some specific actions and put them in context of *when* and *how*. Now, push that context further: I will join a dating site and connect in person with at least one person per week. I will also list the specific people that I want to ask for introductions and give myself a week to have that discussion.

Finally, follow the *Habit Formation Formula* and build in repetition and expansion for each goal. If you anticipate backsliding or procrastination (and you should), write down at least a half-dozen workarounds that will get you back on track, such as having a friend check in on your progress, or creating your own mastermind or accountability group to keep you honest. Although it may sound a bit complicated, once you create the structure and master the process, you'll find yourself identifying and attaining goals like never before.

FEEDING HOPE

In an ideal world, we'd all remain as wonderfully wide eyed about our goals as when we were children. But all too often, the challenges of life rob us of that joyful state. Thankfully, there are people like Amber Michel who are dedicated to providing young people with more than just the necessities of life.

A fifteen-year education professional, Amber now teaches a combination kindergarten and first grade class in the same Sacramento neighborhood where she grew up. The first person in her family to graduate from college, Amber could have gone wherever she wanted to start her career. But she didn't want to be part of the community's past—she wanted to be part of its future.

Not only are her students different ages, but they come from mixed-race, ethnically diverse homes, many living below the poverty line. It's not unusual for a child to come to class having been up all night due to gunshots in the neighborhood or domestic abuse in the next room. They're badly nourished, sleep deprived, and often stressed and scared. By age five, most of the kids know much too much about drug dealers and meth labs. But Amber fervently believes that their present circumstances don't have to dictate their future.

"When I was little, I had a teacher who recognized that there was something special about me," Amber said. "She showed me that I had value. That made me want to become a teacher." While Amber follows the prescribed curriculum with her students, she also wants them to learn the lesson of self-worth. In fact, she's just as concerned about their physical, mental, and emotional well-being as she is their intellectual development. Not easy in a Title I school where kids with lice and scabies are allowed to stay in the classroom because there's simply no place else for them to go during the day. Despite the challenges, Amber is dedicated to teaching her students what it means to envision a better future.

One of the ways she feeds hope, infusing her classroom with a sense of possibility about the future, is to introduce the children to yoga. To accomplish this, Amber brought in my executive assistant, Rachel Kane, who is not only my right hand in business, but also a certified yoga and barre instructor, to teach yoga to the K-first class. The kids all have their own yoga mats and Rachel has taught them the basics, including deep breathing and yoga postures. From plank to goddess pose, they learn to work together without judgement or competition. But Rachel and Amber have also taught them about focus, concentration, relaxation, and problem solving skills they can use for a lifetime.

Most of all, Amber says, she wants them to learn to be responsible for their own needs. If a child needs to stretch during lesson time, she tells him to get up and stretch or go into child's pose. If a kid needs to nap, she tells her to pull out her yoga mat and find a quiet corner. Whatever the children need to do to feel safe and happy, as long as they're not harming anyone else, she encourages them to do.

When I asked Amber what her administration thinks of all this, she replied, "Fortunately, kindergarten is often off in its own little world. My supervisors know things are working because my kids test well and move to the next level. But it's more than that. My students are so excited, so forgiving, and so full of love—exactly what adults should be. I just want them to stay this way."

None of this comes easily or cheaply. Amber pays for yoga (generously discounted by Rachel) and music lessons out of her own pocket, because she believes her kids—and all kids—deserve it. But it's not because she's got a lot of extra time or money. Amber has three children of her own and is also a partner in a local restaurant, Bacon and Butter, where her brother is the chef. She works at the restaurant from 4 am to 7 am each weekday, handling the business end of the business, teaches all day, and then stops by the restaurant again before heading home.

I have no doubt that Amber's dedication to feeding hope—literally and metaphorically—will create an entire generation of loved and loving adults. Here's hoping there are a lot more Ambers out there!

HOPEFUL HABITS

KEY TAKEAWAY #10

Create your True Hope Roadmap by envisioning your ideal future, taking action steps tied to context, and forming habits. Remember, habits rarely hit *automaticity* in twenty-one days, as many of us have been taught, so stick with it until it sticks.

HOPEFUL BELIEF #10

Think about the people who have inspired you on your path. What specific actions did they take that made you feel happy, valued, and hopeful about the future? Reach out to one or all of them and let them know what their inspiration has meant to you over the years.

HOPEFUL BEHAVIOR #10

Decide how you will feed hope into your family, organization, or community. Better yet, determine how you can impact all three of those ecosystems. As specifically as possible, determine the necessary action steps by identifying exactly what you will do and when you will do it. Share your plans with other like-minded people and start feeding hope. The world needs you!

ACKNOWLEDGMENTS

It takes more than a village to write a book. It takes a vast community of loving and knowledgeable friends, family, clients, and colleagues. And while I can never fully thank mine for all the help and support they've given me, I'll do my best. Thanks first to my discerning and talented critics—Lia Ottaviano and Martha Finney—who took this book to a level beyond my own capabilities. Hats off to Lia and everyone at Diversion Books, who understood from the get-go that hope is not an abstract concept but, rather, a way of leading and living. For helping to spread the word about *hope theory*, and this book in particular, thanks to PR gurus Andrea McKinnon and Alexandra Israel. Much gratitude also to my fiction writers' group—Kevin Jones, Alexandra Stewart, and Michael Stewart—who provided thoughtful notes and endless encouragement when I switched over to nonfiction on this literary journey. Next, to my beloved friends and family, who give me more hope and purpose than anyone could wish for: David Stern,

Harrison Gill, Zack Gill, Cameron Chambers, Barbara Burgess, Shela Dean, Belinda Phillips, Carolyn Akel, and Sharon Williams. And a special shout out to my right-hand everything, Rachel Kane, for making my work and life so much richer (and easier!). Finally, to all my hopeful clients who march bravely into an unknown future, ready to transform their dreams of a better world into action. Keep feeding hope—the world needs you!

SUMMARY OF HOPEFUL HABITS

Key Tools and Takeaways

KEY TAKEAWAY #1

Hope is the jet fuel for the journey of work and life. While we've been taught to believe that "hope is not a strategy," hope must be present *before* the application of strategies and resources for us to make full use of the tools that lead to positive change.

HOPEFUL BELIEF #1

Now that we've seen how critical (and scientifically valid) it is to link your current life with your future goals, let's begin to visualize that future self. We can start by putting a twist on the question we've all been asked as kids. Instead of

"*What* do you want to be when you grow up?" ask yourself, "*Who* do you want to be when you grow up?"

What positive personality traits do you currently see in yourself that you'd like to develop over time? These might include being adventurous, intellectually curious, health minded, and/or financially savvy. Now, ask yourself the opposite. What less appealing traits would you like to minimize over time? These could include overspending, bad nutrition or exercise habits, and/or reluctance to go after the promotion or job you want. In other words, begin to imagine the next iteration of you. Be aware of the gap and what you need to do to close it.

HOPEFUL BEHAVIOR #1

Pick one positive trait that you currently see as part of your personality. Now, add an action that would amplify the positive trait. For example, if you said you wanted to develop your intellectual curiosity, you might consider taking a class, attending a seminar, or listening to an audio series that would expand your skills or knowledge.

Next, pick the negative trait you wish to minimize over time. If you determined that your finance savvy is not up to par, pick an action that would begin to build that muscle. Perhaps you'll decide to meet with an investment advisor, overhaul your college or retirement plans, or take a seminar in financial planning. By consciously focusing on your beliefs, both positive and negative, you can begin to determine behaviors to expand and develop your best future self.

KEY TAKEAWAY #2

Though hope has been the subject of scores of poems, myths, and religious texts, the scientific study of hope, or *hope theory*, dates back less than a quarter-century. With Dr. Snyder's creation of the Hope Scale, levels of hopefulness can be measured by empirical means.

While Snyder, with his foundation in positive psychology, defines hope as the combination of goals, agency, and pathways, oncologist Dr. Jerome Groopman looks at hope through a physiological lens, tying belief to behavior to arrive at a desired result.

HOPEFUL BELIEF #2

Think of a past accomplishment of yours. It can be something dating as far back as childhood—like getting a blue ribbon in a swim meet—or it can be something recent, like writing your first guest blog for a colleague's website. What was the belief behind this accomplishment? Did the idea of winning inspire you to take on the hard work of regular swim practices? What about writing the guest blog? Is it part of a larger vision of creating your own platform? Of becoming a writer?

HOPEFUL BEHAVIOR #2

Identify the belief that drove your behavior toward the positive outcome you experienced. Did you win a blue ribbon because you enjoy athletics, like being part of a team, or love the feeling of winning? It could, of course, be all of these things, but see if you can pinpoint the primary underlying belief that got you into action. If you said, "competition," how can you apply your competitive spirit to another goal? To several goals? Try to muster that fabulous feeling you had of winning that swim meet as you tackle your next goal.

KEY TAKEAWAY #3

As the workplace changes with unprecedented speed and complexity, it is critical for emerging and established leaders to recognize what tomorrow's workplace will look like, so they can begin to prepare today. By consciously linking beliefs to workplace behaviors, you'll be much more likely to speed up your growth curve.

HOPEFUL BELIEF #3

Think about a change you'd like to make at your workplace. It should be specific, measurable, and significant or it's unlikely you—and others—will want to stick with it. Like the executive who used her influence to start a national women's leadership initiative at Kellogg's. Or Jessica, who turned March Madness into a networking opportunity.

Next, think about yourself as *Employee Zero*. Do you have the influence to make this change happen on your own? Or do you need someone with more clout to champion your idea? If so, who would that be? How will you describe the desired change to your leadership or to your *Employee Zero Supporter*?

HOPEFUL BEHAVIOR #3

Now, take the first step. Write out your change story. What problem would it solve? Who would benefit? How difficult would it be to initiate? How would you communicate the change and how will you make it stick? What obstacles or pushback can you expect?

Once you've gotten your story as fine-tuned as possible, go pitch it directly to management as *Employee Zero*, or sell it to a potential *Employee Zero Supporter* who can get on board and help you make it happen.

KEY TAKEAWAY #4

Teams are an essential construct of the workplace, but they can drain hopefulness, eventually affecting the entire organization. It is up to the team leader to keep the interaction positive and productive. Research shows that *how* teams communicate can often be as important as *what* they communicate.

HOPEFUL BELIEF #4

Take a look at the personalities described in *The Personality of High-Performance Teams* section above. What's your personality type? Can you identify the types of other people on your team? Is there a good mix, or are there too many of one type and not enough of another? How might you change the group to enhance productivity?

HOPEFUL BEHAVIOR #4

Even if you don't have MIT's electronic badge system to monitor team communication, you can determine how well it's working. Designate someone to be an observer and, if you want to keep this exercise under wraps until you've completed it, identify them as your notetaker. Have them sit in on a typical group meeting and record their observations on the *Five Factors of Effective Team Communication.* Are all team members talking and listening in equal measure? Do they face one another when they speak? Are they connecting with each other, including side conversations, and not just with the leader? Do they explore outside the group and share their insights?

Let your team know what you've learned about team communication and how *energy, engagement*, and *exploration* lead to success. Next, share your observations about your team and how you can improve your interactions. And, don't forget the fun!

KEY TAKEAWAY #5

Whether you're a new or seasoned leader, you need to know what your organization wants from you in terms of meeting business objectives, but you also need to understand what your followers want: trust, compassion, stability, and hope.

HOPEFUL BELIEF #5

Look back through this chapter to determine your *Leadership Superpower.* Are you a technology-driven leader?

A leader who connects deeply with others? Maybe you're a great communicator or analyst. Write down what makes you truly great at what you do—and don't hold back. This is your time to shine a spotlight on your superhero strength.

HOPEFUL BEHAVIOR #5

Next, identify three actions that would make even greater use of your superpower. Determine a specific outcome (or outcomes) you want to achieve, and laser-focus your strengths and skills right at the core. Maybe you'll organize an off-site event to give everyone the latest tech updates to improve their productivity. Perhaps you'll use your communication super skills to kick off a new company newsletter or intranet. Whatever you decide to do, shift your superpower to high gear and get moving.

KEY TAKEAWAY #6

The essence of effective communication is that the message you deliver is the same as the message that is received. Simple, but not necessarily easy. Practice this skill, and it will enhance everything you do in both personal and professional life.

HOPEFUL BELIEF #6

Assess your own communication skills, noting one key strength and one area of improvement. Share your thoughts with at least three colleagues and see if they agree or disagree with your assessment. Ask them how they think you can improve as a communicator.

HOPEFUL BEHAVIOR #6

Assign yourself a communication stretch goal based on the feedback you received. Join your local Toastmasters group or offer to give a presentation at work. Also try practicing the A-B-A communication process by ending every conversation in which information is exchanged or an agreement is reached with a clear, agreed-upon summary statement.

KEY TAKEAWAY #7

Despite an increase in career advancement for women professionals over the past twenty years, progress has been slow, and subconscious gender biases are a major factor. We all experience prejudice and bias, based largely on our culture, education, and personal history. It's our job as emerging and established leaders to level the playing field in terms of recruitment, management, and advancement.

HOPEFUL BELIEF #7

Get a gut check on your strengths and weaknesses so you'll have the confidence—and objective data—to defeat, or at least lessen, gender bias and inequality when you encounter them. Do a self-inventory of what you consider your biggest assets as well as your most pressing areas for improvement. Now, see if you can identity your own biases about women in the workplace and gender equality.

HOPEFUL BEHAVIOR #7

Next, ask five trusted colleagues to provide three descriptive words or phrases in answer to the questions: "What do you think are my three greatest strengths?" and "What do you think are three areas where I could improve my performance?" Reconcile the feedback with how you feel about your own work, making sure not to downplay your accomplishments. Decide which improvement you want to tackle first, and get going!

KEY TAKEAWAY #8

While it's convenient to categorize people in terms of generational frameworks, it can often lead to false stereotypes and restrictions. Instead, when we look past the clichés and see people as individuals, we get a much better sense of their unique gifts and challenges, hopes and dreams.

HOPEFUL BELIEF #8

Think about the people you know from each of the generational groups outlined above—Traditionalists, Baby Boomers, Gen Xers, Millennials, and Gen Z. Are there stereotypes that you assign to these individuals just by virtue of their age group? What are the stereotypes you hold? How accurate do you think they are? Now, consider your own generational cohort. What stereotypes do people hold about you and your generational counterparts? Are any of them true? If not, how do you challenge them?

HOPEFUL BEHAVIOR #8

Choose someone from another generation that you can partner with to exchange knowledge and expertise. If you're a Millennial, what might you hope to learn from a Traditionalist or Boomer? Conversely, if you're a Boomer, what insights or information could a Gen Xer or Millennial share that would be helpful to your growth? Now, go have the conversation with that person to structure a satisfying cross-generational partnership. If you have a number of close relationships, consider modeling the Okinawan "moais," finding 3-5 people who will all agree to help each other by sharing positive beliefs, skills, support, and feedback.

KEY TAKEAWAY #9

Despite the extreme challenges of failing health, chronic homelessness, and crippling mental illness, there is hope. From recognizing the issue to changing your mindset to creating a support network, life can improve. The remarkable role models cited in this chapter shared some simple things you can do to help.

HOPEFUL BELIEF #9

Imagine a day in your life as a person who is homeless and suffering from poor physical or mental health. Take yourself through the entire day, from waking up on the street or in a shelter to finding food, bathroom facilities, and a place to sleep at night. How would your day be different?

What would you miss most? Would you feel ashamed? Frightened? Resigned? Where would you turn for help?

HOPEFUL BEHAVIOR #9

Pick one action you can take that would benefit a member or members of this fragile population. Will you volunteer in a shelter or soup kitchen? Take a homeless person to a coffee shop for lunch? Give some relief to a friend or family member who is a primary caregiver by offering to cook a meal, do the laundry, or sit in for them so they can run errands or take a nap? How will you be a messenger of hope?

KEY TAKEAWAY #10

Create your True Hope Roadmap by envisioning your ideal future, taking action steps tied to context, and forming habits. Remember, habits rarely hit *automaticity* in twenty-one days, as many of us have been taught, so stick with it until it sticks.

HOPEFUL BELIEF #10

Think about the people who have inspired you on your path. What specific actions did they take that made you feel happy, valued, and hopeful about the future? Reach out to one or all of them and let them know what their inspiration has meant to you over the years.

HOPEFUL BEHAVIOR #10

Decide how you will feed hope into your family, organization, or community. Better yet, determine how you can impact all three of those ecosystems. As specifically as possible, determine the necessary action steps by identifying exactly what you will do and when you will do it. Share your plans with other like-minded people and start feeding hope. The world needs you!

LIBBY GILL & COMPANY

About Libby's Coaching and Consulting Services

How do you re-energize an executive who is struggling with change? How can you inspire risk-taking in a team that is clinging to the status quo? What can you do to infuse your leaders—and future leaders—with vitality and vision?

Give them the greatest gift of all: hope.

Hope, which derives from Old English and means "to leap forward with expectation," is based on the *belief* that change is possible and the *expectation* that an individual's actions can result in a better future. It's the difference between people who give up in the face of change and those who rise to every challenge, no matter how seemingly insurmountable.

Providing a proven methodology, executive coach and

bestselling author Libby Gill guides senior executives and rising stars to professional success. The foundation for her process comes from her ongoing study of the impact of hopefulness in the workplace, as well as documented research from the medical and psychological communities, as seen in this book.

In short, Libby helps executives change their beliefs so they can change their behaviors. First, Libby guides Clients to increase their level of hopefulness through deep exploration into core beliefs and character. Then, she provides the essential tools of coaching, including assessments, development plans, ongoing sessions, and more.

Through more than thirty years motivating and managing professionals, Libby has seen that it is critical to 1) increase hopefulness and 2) provide strategic tools—in that order, and not the other way around. Attempting to change behaviors without first changing beliefs is like giving someone a power drill without electricity—completely ineffective.

WHAT IS THE COACHING PROCESS?

Now that "do more with less" has become the business norm, many executives and managers are pulled in multiple, sometimes conflicting, directions as they attempt to stretch their limited manpower and resources. As they struggle with bottom-line expectations, staff reductions, a disengaged workforce, globalization, and more, is it any wonder they have little time left over for their own professional growth? Even the most motivated managers are often forced to let their leadership potential and skills enhancement slide while dealing with more pressing issues.

That's where executive coaching can fill the gap. Coaching gives executives the permission—if only for one hour a week—to focus on their own growth with the guidance of an objective outside expert. Libby specializes in working with executives and managers in these core groups:

- New leaders
- Senior management
- Women executives
- Executives experiencing challenges

Coaching generally takes place via regularly scheduled phone calls, in person, or a combination of the two. But it doesn't stop there. Libby will do whatever is necessary to take your executive or team to their highest potential. The process generally starts with in-person interviews so Libby can create a customized 360 Assessment by interviewing key staff and stakeholders about the Client's performance, then design a program of ongoing coaching to achieve specific behavioral outcomes.

Libby offers a complimentary coaching session so the Client may learn more about the coaching process and see if Libby's style is a fit for their needs and temperament. Coaching may be held by phone, Skype, or in person. The coaching process includes, but is not limited to, the following:

- 360 Assessments
- Personal Development Plan

- Scheduled coaching calls
- As-needed attention via phone, email, or Skype
- Regular team interaction
- Unlimited email access
- Access to any of Libby's public events and seminars
- A copy of any of Libby's books

WHAT ARE THE BENEFITS OF COACHING?

By raising the Client's hope level and then providing strategic tools at precisely the right moment in the process, Libby is able to help Clients increase their confidence and competence. She provides a broad range of tools customized to the individual's needs and adapted to their optimal learning style to help them:

1. Clarify their vision of personal and professional success
2. Simplify the most direct route to realizing core objectives
3. Execute their personal Developmental Action Plan against measurable milestones for success (or "wins along the way")

Coaching will guide executives to achieve the following (and more depending on their unique situation):

- Develop their leadership style and executive presence
- Understand how beliefs drive behavior

- Gain self-confidence
- Challenge limiting assumptions
- Establish priorities
- Learn to communicate and present more persuasively
- Create a polished personal brand within the company and industry
- Positively motivate others to excel
- Determine factors for accountability
- Collaborate effectively and foster team building
- Build loyalty and engagement
- Increase balance between work and home

CUSTOMIZED TRAINING OPTIONS

Libby also offers customized training in specific skill areas, designed for high-potential candidates through senior-level executives. After an initial conversation to discuss challenges and objectives, Libby will create a custom curriculum for your group. Libby generally conducts advance research and pre-interviews with key stakeholders and team members to maximize results.

With more than thirty years of experience in all aspects of communications, Libby is able to create custom content for your group, designed to fit the learning needs and cultural tone. She employs exercises and training methods ranging from C-level keynote messaging to comedy improvisation to engage participants and ensure outcomes.

Areas of expertise include:

- Communications skills building
- Presentation and platform skills
- Personal branding
- Message training
- Team trust and collaboration
- Creativity and innovation

WHY CHOOSE LIBBY?

After nearly twenty years in senior leadership roles at media giants Universal, Sony, and Turner Broadcasting, as well as serving as the PR/branding brain behind the launch of the *Dr. Phil Show,* Libby founded Los Angeles-based coaching and consulting firm Libby Gill & Company in 2000. A sought-after media guest, Libby has shared her success strategies on CNN, MSNBC, NPR, the Today Show, and in *BusinessWeek, O Magazine, Self, Time, The New York Times, Wall Street Journal,* and others.

Author of four previous books, Libby chronicled her journey of overcoming the negative self-perceptions of having grown up in a family plagued by alcoholism, divorce, mental illness, and suicide in *Traveling Hopefully: How to Lose Your Family Baggage and Jumpstart Your Life.* Business leaders, including Zappos.com CEO Tony Hsieh and Dr. Ken Blanchard, have endorsed Libby's award-winning book *You Unstuck: Mastering the New Rules of Risk-taking in Work and Life.* Libby's last book, *Capture the Mindshare and the Market Share Will Follow,* shows readers how to create deep and lasting connections based on authentic value.

BIBLIOGRAPHY

American Management Association. "The Myth of Generational Differences in the Workplace." *American Management Association.* Accessed July 1, 2017. http://www.amanet.org/training/articles/ the-myth-of-generational-differences-in-the-workplace.aspx.

AON. "How Can We Beat Unconscious Gender Bias In The Workplace?" *The One Brief.* Accessed July 1, 2017. http://www.theonebrief.com/ how-can-we-beat-unconscious-gender-bias-in-the-workplace/.

Associated Press. "Swedish Cinemas Take Aim at Gender Bias with Bechdel Test Rating." *The Guardian*, November 6, 2013. https:// www.theguardian.com/world/2013/nov/06/swedish-cinemas -bechdel-test-films-gender-bias.

Australian Aged Care Quality Agency. "Bucket List Program." *Australian Aged Care Quality Agency.* Accessed July 1, 2017. https://www.aacqa.gov.au/providers/promoting-quality/ better-practice-awards/2014-better-practice-award-winners/ bucket-list-program.

Bambenek, Cadence. "Looking to Help Refugees, This Design Student Created Jackets That Transform into Tents and Sleeping Bags." *Business Insider*, July 11, 2016. http://www.businessinsider.com/

angela-luna-designs-jackets-to-help-syrian-refugees-2016-7/#luna-emphasized-that-the-collection-isnt-inspired-by-refugees-but-its-intended-to-help-them-by-looking-at-their-needs-and-trying-to-address-those-through-design.

Bhargava, Rohit. *Likeonomics: The Unexpected Truth Behind Earning Trust, Influencing Behavior, and Inspiring Action.* Hoboken, NJ: John Wiley & Sons, Inc., 2012.

Boedker, Christina. "The Rise of the Compassionate Leader: Should You Be Cruel to Be Kind?" *BusinessThink*, August 21, 2012. https://www.businessthink.unsw.edu.au/Pages/The-Rise-of-the-Compassionate-Leader--Should-You-Be-Cruel-to-Be-Kind.aspx.

Box Office Mojo. "Superhero." *Box Office Mojo.* Accessed July 1, 2017. http://www.boxofficemojo.com/genres/chart/?id=superhero.htm&sort=opengross&order=DESC&p=.html.

Buchanan, Wil. "The Younger Generation Has Been Ruining The World Since Forever." *Ambitious*, July 24, 2015. http://ambitious.actthreeassociates.com/the-younger-generation-has-been-ruining-the-world-since-forever/.

Buettner, Dan. "Power 9." *Blue Zones*, November 10, 2016. https://bluezones.com/2016/11/power-9/.

The Blue Zones: Lessons for Living Longer From the People Who've Lived the Longest. Washington, DC: National Geographic Society, 2008.

Camarote, Robin. "How to Make Powerful Changes at Work by Being 'Employee Zero.'" *Inc.*, July 27, 2016. https://www.inc.com/robin-camarote/how-to-make-powerful-changes-at-work-by-being-employee-zero.html.

Clear, James. "Achieve Your Goals: The Simple Trick That Doubles Your Odds of Success." *James Clear.* Accessed July 31, 2017. http://jamesclear.com/implementation-intentions.

Covey, Stephen M.R. *The Speed of Trust: The One Thing That Changes Everything.* New York: Free Press, 2006.

Cross, Rob, Reb Rebele, and Adam Grant. "Collaborative Overload." *Harvard Business Review*, February 2016. https://hbr.org/2016/01/collaborative-overload.

Damour, Lisa. "Asking Girls and Boys, What Would Wonder Woman Do?" *The New York Times*, June 8, 2017. https://mobile.nytimes.com/2017/06/08/well/family/asking-girls-and-boys-what-would-wonder-woman-do.html?smid=tw-share&_r=0&referer=https%3A%2F%2Ft.co%2FV4LsFNOZn6.

Dickinson, Emily. "Hope is the thing with feathers (254)." https://www.poets.org/poetsorg/poem/hope-thing-feathers-254.

Duhigg, Charles. "What Google Learned From Its Quest to Build the Perfect Team." *The New York Times Magazine*, February 25, 2016. https://www.nytimes.com/2016/02/28/magazine/what-google-learned-from-its-quest-to-build-the-perfect-team.html?_r=0.

EY. "Global Generations: A Global Study on Work-Life Challenges across Generations." EY, 2015. http://www.ey.com/Publication/vwLUAssets/EY-global-generations-a-global-study-on-work-life-challenges-across-generations/$FILE/EY-global-generations-a-global-study-on-work-life-challenges-across-generations.pdf.

Finkelstein, Stacey R., and Ayelet Fishbach. "Tell Me What I Did Wrong: Experts Seek and Respond to Negative Feedback." *Journal of Consumer Research* 39, no. 1 (June 2012): 22–38.

Framingham Heart Study. "History of the Framingham Heart Study." *Framingham Heart Study*. Accessed July 1, 2017. https://www.framinghamheartstudy.org/about-fhs/history.php.

Frankl, Victor E. *Man's Search for Meaning*. Boston: Beacon Press, 2006.

Fredrickson, Barbara L. *Positivity: Top-Notch Research Reveals the Upward Spiral That Will Change Your Life*. New York: Three Rivers Press, 2009.

Gardner, Benjamin, Phillippa Lally, and Jane Wardle. "Making Health Habitual: The Psychology of 'habit-Formation' and General Practice." *The British Journal of General Practice* 62, no. 605 (December 2012): 664–66. doi:10.3399/bjgp12X659466.

Garner, Bryan A. *HBR Guide to Better Business Writing*. HBR Guide Series. Boston: Harvard Business Review Press, 2012.

Gielan, Michelle. *Broadcasting Happiness: The Science of Igniting and Sustaining Positive Change*. Dallas: BenBella Books, Inc., 2015.

Gollwitzer, Peter M., Paschal Sheeran, Verena Michalski, and Andrea E. Seifert. "When Intentions Go Public: Does Social Reality Widen the Intention-Behavior Gap?" *Psychological Science* 20, no. 5 (2009): 612–18.

Goman, Carol Kinsey. "Great Leaders Are Positively Infectious." *Forbes*, July 11, 2012. https://www.forbes.com/sites/carolkinsey-goman/2012/07/11/great-leaders-are-positively-infectious/#2f551ed578cc.

Grant, Adam. *Give and Take: Why Helping Others Drives Our Success*. Penguin Books, 2014.

Groopman, Jerome. *The Anatomy of Hope: How People Prevail in the Face of Illness*. New York: Random House, 2004.

Halter, Jeffery Tobias. "The Barriers to Advancing Women: What Men Aren't Seeing." *SmartBrief*, September 13, 2016. http://www.smartbrief.com/original/2016/09/barriers-advancing-women-what-men-arent-seeing?utm_source=brief.

Heikkila, Andrew. "Jobs That Don't Exist Yet: How to Prepare for the Future of Work." *Business 2 Community*, March 16, 2016. http://www.business2community.com/human-resources/jobs-dont-exist-yet-prepare-future-work-01484828#ftRw3sSokdWymkeS.97.

Henry, Meghan, Rian Watt, Lily Rosenthal, and Azim Shivji. "The 2016 Annual Homeless Assessment Report (AHAR) to Congress." The U.S. Department of Housing and Urban Development, November 2016. https://www.hudexchange.info/resources/documents/2016-AHAR-Part-1.pdf.

Hewlett, Sylvia Ann, Kerrie Peraino, Laura Sherbin, and Karen Sumberg. "The Sponsor Effect: Breaking Through the Last Glass Ceiling." *Harvard Business Review*, January 12, 2011.

Jean-Louis, Jardley. *How to Keep Getting Great Employee Feedback as Your Company Grows*. Video. The Playbook, 2017. https://www.inc.com/video/jessica-mah/how-to-keep-getting-great-employee-feedback-as-your-company-grows.html.

Kirkham, Elyssa. "1 in 3 Americans Has Saved $0 for Retirement." *Money*, March 14, 2016. http://time.com/money/4258451/retirement-savings-survey/.

Kristof, Nicholas. "When Women Rule." *The New York Times*, February 10, 2008. http://www.nytimes.com/2008/02/10/opinion/10kristof.html.

Lagerberg, Francesca. "The Value of Diversity." *GrantThornton*, September 29, 2015. https://www.grantthornton.global/en/insights/articles/diverse-boards-in-india-uk-and-us-outperform-male-only-peers-by-us$655bn/.

Lancaster, Lynne C., and David Stillman. *When Generations Collide: Who They Are. Why They Clash. How to Solve the Generational Puzzle at Work.* New York: HarperBusiness, 2002.

LasVegasSun. *Hip Op-Eration*. YouTube video, 2013. https://www.youtube.com/watch?v=GAKEwkhlB_M.

Lopez, Shane J. *Making Hope Happen: Create the Future You Want for Yourself and Others*. New York: Atria Paperback, 2013.

Lyons, Dan. "Jerks and the Start-Ups They Ruin." *The New York Times*,

April 1, 2017. https://www.nytimes.com/2017/04/01/opinion/sunday/jerks-and-the-start-ups-they-ruin.html.

Mayer, John D. "How to Plan for Your Future Self." *Scientific American*, March 1, 2014. https://www.scientificamerican.com/article/how-to-plan-for-your-future-self/.

———. *Personal Intelligence: The Power of Personality and How It Shapes Our Lives*. New York: Scientific American/Farrar, Straus and Giroux, 2014.

McClintock, Pamela. "'Wonder Woman' Box Office: Where It Ranks in the Superhero Pantheon." *The Hollywood Reporter*, June 4, 2017. http://www.hollywoodreporter.com/heat-vision/wonder-woman-box-office-ranks-superhero-pantheon-1010063.

Meehan, Mary. "The Perfect Name For The Next Generation Of Americans." *Forbes*, April 15, 2014. https://www.forbes.com/sites/marymeehan/2014/04/15/the-perfect-name-for-the-next-generation-of-americans/#b14a5bf34162.

Memory Care Support. "Memory Care Support." *Memory Care Support*. Accessed July 1, 2017. https://memorycaresupport.com.

Mental Health America. "Mental Health America." *Mental Health America*. Accessed July 1, 2017. http://www.mentalhealthamerica.net.

NAMI. "Mental Health By The Numbers." *NAMI*. Accessed July 1, 2017. https://www.nami.org/Learn-More/Mental-Health-By-the-Numbers#sthash.KiuKpUfm.dpuf.

———. "NAMI." *NAMI*. Accessed July 1, 2017. https://www.nami.org/#.

National Alliance to End Homelessness. "Cronically Homeless." *National Alliance to End Homelessness*. Accessed July 1, 2017. http://endhomelessness.org/homelessness-in-america/who-experiences-homelessness/chronically-homeless/.

Nierenberg, Gerard I., and Henry H. Calero. *How to Read a Person Like a Book*. New York: Pocket Books, 1971.

Pentland, Alex "Sandy." "The New Science of Building Great Teams." *Harvard Business Review*, April 2012. https://hbr.org/2012/04/the-new-science-of-building-great-teams.

Plous, S. "Understanding Prejudice." *Implicit Association Test*. Accessed July 1, 2017. http://www.understandingprejudice.org/iat/index2.htm.

Quinn, Ben. "Migrant Death Toll Passes 5,000 after Two Boats Capsize off Italy." *The Guardian*, December 23, 2016. https://www.theguardian.com/world/2016/dec/23/record-migrant-death-toll-two-boats-capsize-italy-un-refugee.

Ranker Community. "The Best Comic Book Superheroes of All

Time." *Ranker*. Accessed July 1, 2017. http://www.ranker.com/crowdranked-list/best-superheroes-all-time.

Rath, Tom, and Barry Conchie. *Strengths Based Leadership: Great Leaders, Teams, and Why People Follow*. New York: Gallup Press, 2008.

Rice, Curt. "How Blind Auditions Help Orchestras to Eliminate Gender Bias." *The Guardian*, October 14, 2013. https://www.theguardian.com/women-in-leadership/2013/oct/14/blind-auditions-orchestras-gender-bias.

Robb, Alice. "Why Men Are Prone to Interrupting Women." *The New York Times*, March 19, 2015. http://nytlive.nytimes.com/womenintheworld/2015/03/19/google-chief-blasted-for-repeatedly-interrupting-female-government-official/.

Sarda-Joshi, Gauri. "Dunning-Kruger Effect: Why You're Not As Smart As You Think." *Brain Fodder*. Accessed July 1, 2017. http://brainfodder.org/dunning-kruger-effect/.

Snyder, C.R. *The Psychology of Hope: You Can Get Here from There*. New York: The Free Press, 1994.

Snyder, C.R., S.C. Sympson, F.C. Ybasco, T.F. Borders, M.A. Babyak, and R.L. Higgins. "Development and Validation of the State Hope Scale." *Journal of Personality and Social Psychology* 70 (1996): 321–35.

Stern, Stephen L., R. Dhanda, and H.P. Hazuda. "Hopelessness Predicts Mortality in Older Mexican and European Americans." *Psychosomatic Medicine* 63, no. 3 (June 2001): 344–51.

Szabo, Liz. "Cost of Not Caring: Nowhere to Go." *USA Today*. Accessed July 1, 2017. https://www.usatoday.com/story/news/nation/2014/05/12/mental-health-system-crisis/7746535/.

Tanner, Robert. "Understanding and Managing the 4 Generations in the Workplace." *Management Is a Journey*, June 28, 2016. https://managementisajourney.com/understanding-and-managing-the-4-generations-in-the-workplace/.

TEDx Talks. *Design Intervention For Global Issues*. YouTube video, 2016. https://www.youtube.com/watch?v=t0FljT15Dvs.

"The Dallas Street Choir Makes Historic Carnegie Hall Debut." Online radio recording. *All Things Considered*. NPR, June 14, 2017. http://www.npr.org/2017/06/14/532959314/the-dallas-street-choir-makes-historic-carnegie-hall-debut.

The Hip Op-eration Foundation. "The Hip Op-Eration Crew." *The Hip Op-Eration Crew*. Accessed July 1, 2017. http://www.hipop-eration.com.

The Jason Foundation. "Facts & Stats." *The Jason Foundation*.

Accessed July 1, 2017. http://jasonfoundation.com/youth-suicide/facts-stats/.

The Pursuit of Happiness. "Ed Diener." *The Pursuit of Happiness.* Accessed July 1, 2017. http://www.pursuit-of-happiness.org/history-of-happiness/ed-diener/.

Toastmasters International. "Toastmasters International." *Toastmasters International.* Accessed July 1, 2017. http://www.toastmasters.org.

Torres, Nicole. "Most People Don't Want to Be Managers." *Harvard Business Review*, September 18, 2014. https://hbr.org/2014/09/most-people-dont-want-to-be-managers.

Troksa, Lauren M. "The Study of Generations: A Timeless Notion within a Contemporary Context." Undergraduate Honors Thesis, University of Colorado Boulder, 2016. http://scholar.colorado.edu/cgi/viewcontent.cgi?article=2273&context=honr_theses.

Uniting. *Finding the Why; Enabling Active Participation in Life in Aged Care.* YouTube video, 2014. https://www.youtube.com/watch?v=hZN1CyEiFNM.

Walsh, Bryan. "Alan Kurdi's Story: Behind The Most Heartbreaking Photo of 2015." *TIME*, December 29, 2015. http://time.com/4162306/alan-kurdi-syria-drowned-boy-refugee-crisis/.

Wilding, Josh. "10 Greatest Marvel And DC Comics Superheroes Of All-Time." *ComicBookMovie.com*, March 13, 2016. https://www.comicbookmovie.com/comics/marvel_comics/10-greatest-marvel-and-dc-comics-superheroes-of-all-time-a132032.

Woetzel, Jonathan, Anu Madgavkar, Kweilin Ellingrud, Eric Labaye, Sandrine Devillard, Eric Kutcher, James Manyika, Richard Dobbs, and Mekala Kirshnan. "How Advancing Women's Equality Can Add $12 Trillion to Global Growth." *McKinsey & Company*, September 2015. http://www.mckinsey.com/global-themes/employment-and-growth/how-advancing-womens-equality-can-add-12-trillion-to-global-growth.

Yee, Lareina, Alexis Krivkovich, Eric Kutcher, Blair Epstein, Rachel Thomas, Ashley Finch, Marianne Cooper, and Ellen Konar. "Women in the Workplace 2016." Lean In and McKinsey & Company, n.d.

Your Body Language May Shape Who You Are. TED Video. TED, 2012. https://www.ted.com/talks/amy_cuddy_your_body_language_shapes_who_you_are.

Zenger Folkman. "Zenger Folkman Likability Index." Zenger Folkman,

2013. http://www.zengerfolkman.com/media/articles/ZFCo-WP-Likability-Index-040413.pdf.

Zipkin, Nina. "The Success of 'Wonder Woman' Speaks Volumes About Opportunity." *Entrepreneur*, June 6, 2017. https://www.entrepreneur.com/article/295384.